With Kind regards And best wishes
& continued 'World-Class Performance
in all of your chosen endeavors

WORLD-CLASS
PERFORMANCE

THE COMMITMENT; THE PURSUIT; THE ACHIEVEMENT

MICHAEL G. WINSTON

Best,

Mitch G. Winston

1620 SW 5TH Avenue

Pompano Beach, FL 33060

ISBN: 978-0-9862641-4-6

LCCN: 2015931058

Printed in the USA

First Edition, 2015

PRAISE FOR WORLD-CLASS PERFORMANCE

"Michael Winston cares very much about leaders who care, and how that caring translates into transformational change in an organization. In *World-Class Performance*, he sheds new and needed light in this arena. This is a big, intelligent work in a small, digestible package. Bravo!"

—David Allen

Best-selling Author, *Getting Things Done: the Art of Stress-Free Productivity*

"From his deep roots in designing and delivering world-class corporate leadership development programs, Michael Winston has created a master-piece book that covers both the principles and practices of high performance in the context of any competitive arena—an Olympic achievement worthy of a Gold medal!"

—Ken Shelton

Founding editor/publisher, *Leadership Excellence*, 1984–2014
Key Writer of *7 Habits of Highly Effective People*, an all-time bestseller
(over 20 million copies sold in 38 languages worldwide)

"Winston captures the spirit of the Olympics and demonstrates how that spirit can lead to lessons learned that may apply in modern organizations. He masterfully transfers insights from Olympic heroes into daily management actions. His examples elegantly reveal how world class performance can occur in both the Olympics and in organizations."

—Dave Ulrich

Professor, Ross School of Business, University of Michigan
Partner, the RBL Group
Ranked #1 most influential person in HR by *HR Magazine*

"The book *World-Class Performance* by Michael Winston is a must-read for everyone in business and government. Michael addresses all of the key elements in building world-class organizations. Leadership through vision and strategy. Setting reach-out goals. Hire the best and the brightest. These are part of many focused strategies necessary to build a world-class organization. Michael's ability to focus on issues so important to all companies and bring his point home is amazing!"

—Mort Topfer

Chairman of the Board, Castletop Capital, LLC
Former Vice-Chairman of the Board, Dell, Inc.
Former Corporate Executive Vice President and Sector President of Motorola, Inc.

"BRAVO!! BRAVO!! APPLAUSE!!! APPLAUSE!!! A great work by a great man!! I am honored to endorse such a very fine piece of work. Michael Winston has given us an original take on the leadership prescription for the ages. A must-read for current and emerging leaders. I look forward to gifting my clients and friends with this book come the New Year."

—James Belasco

Founder of San Diego State University's Management Development Center
Co-Founder of the Financial Times Knowledge Dialogue
International bestselling author and a leading authority in change leadership

"Michael Winston's new book, *World-Class Performance*, arrives just in time for leaders looking for time-tested strategies that work. With the heart of a storyteller, the mind of a superb organizational strategist and the insight of a master practitioner, Michael has written a powerful and compelling book on leadership. With his passion and perspective, Michael proves to be the quintessential storyteller on leadership and corporate best-practices. This book is a *must-read.*"

—Beverly Kaye

Founder and Chairwoman of Career Systems International, Inc.
International bestselling author and leading authority on workplace performance

"Talented athletes become Olympians when their dedicated daily practice platforms a vision of successful performance. Michael Winston eloquently parallels such sports excellence with the essentials of Heroic Corporate Leadership that always win the race for enduring, transformational change across all businesses and institutions. He reveals the strategies of change that integrate courage, confidence, and commitment into practical tactics for operationalizing a leader's highest personal Values. This is a fine book filled with focused inspiration. Read it. Learn from it. Use it in your race to the top."

—Philip Zimbardo, PhD

Author of *The Lucifer Effect, The Time Paradox* and *The Time Cure*
Professor Emeritus, Stanford University
Recipient of American Psychological Association Gold Medal for Lifetime Achievement

"The best leaders of today exemplify the qualities of our present day Olympians. They each represent our hopes and dreams. They inspire us to new heights, to execute faster and be strong in our resolve. Michael Winston connects the traits necessary for Olympic calibre leaders to climb their own Gold medal podium."

—Vince Poscente
Olympic skier, went an incredible 135 mph
Two-time national champion; five-time national speed champion
New York Times bestselling author of *The Age of Speed*

"*World-Class Performance* is a Gold medal achievement, reminding us of the unique, sometimes amazing, and often untapped potential that resides in everyone."

—Joseph G. Cutcliffe, PhD
Founder, Cutcliffe Consulting Group
Key member of Technical Advisory Committee on Testing (TACT) for the State of California and the Advisory Council of the California School of Professional Psychology

"Over the years, I have personally experienced Michael's own unbridled enthusiasm for leadership excellence and his ability to inspire leaders to embrace the essence of change. As a leader, I have moved from the corporate to community service environment, which requires the same relentless pursuit of leadership excellence described herein…with the added challenge of engaging an entire community in building support for a worthy cause. I thank Michael for his wisdom and continual encouragement to always have compassion and commitment for what I do. I thank Michael for compiling this roadmap for leadership success and sharing it with us—like an award-winning fine wine, chock full of a hugely successful combination of grapes and techniques, for all of us to imbibe."

—Suzanne Browning
Executive Director, Kemple Memorial Children's Dental Clinic
Retired after thirty-five-year career as senior executive with The Boeing
Company/McDonnell Douglas (1965–2000)

"I have had the distinct opportunity of working with Michael Winston for many years and have found his integrity and observational skill to be equal to his high intellect and wisdom. Michael's book warrants an Olympic Gold Medal."

—Richard Wintermantel, JD
Consultant, Speaker, and Leadership Team Facilitator.
Retired Executive Officer, Motorola, Inc.

"There are no bad businesses; just management teams through lack of vision and leadership that fail to exploit the opportunity that lies before them. Walmart thrived while Sears failed. The difference was leadership. Michael uses the background of the Olympics to tease out what differentiates the best from the rest. It's not just a book; it's a potentially life-changing experience."

—John E. Major

President of MTSG and advisor of Northwater Capital and Brainlike, Inc.
Former Chief Executive Officer of Novatel Wireless Inc.
Former Chief Executive Officer, Corporate Executive Vice President of Qualcomm, Inc.

"Michael Winston has seen the destruction caused by dishonest and selfish leaders. His own courage and honesty are legendary. He has written a great book about what it really takes to build a great company and a great career. With numerous examples, *World-Class Performance* shows us that leadership excellence is not about posturing and promotion, it's about honesty and willingness to balance commitment to vision with willingness to hear dissent. It's about serving others while demanding more of yourself. I am a better leader for having read it."

—Gifford Pinchot

President, Bainbridge Graduate Institute
American entrepreneur, noted bestselling author
Co-founder of the Bainbridge Graduate Institute

"In many cases, an Olympic Athlete's entire performance and the results of their work are calculated in just a few short minutes. *World-Class Performance* outlines the strong correlation between Olympians and the business world, including the skills and traits needed to succeed. Even more compelling, Michael Winston astutely enlightens us that the most crucial distinctions of an Olympian are often the very same things that are overlooked in business. He reminds us that skills alone are not enough to win, and how crucial it is to focus on the key principles and preparation for the short race and planning for the many ones that will follow."

—Michael Morelli,
Former executive, Eastman Kodak Company

"I worked with Michael Winston many times during his years at Motorola. He is a champion at developing leaders and a winning culture. In *World-Class Performance*, you will find the parallels among the examples of Gold medal–winning athletes and great business success stories."

—Peter Vidmar
Olympic Champion
Chairman of the Board of USA Gymnastics

To my daughter and son, Chelsie and David,

the loves of my life

Contents

ACKNOWLEDGMENTS

The ideas for this book started forming after I watched the closing ceremonies of the 2012 London Olympic Games and continued until months after the close of the 2014 Winter Olympic Games in Sochi, Russia. I was moved by the spectacle of seeing the best in the world give everything they have to win. I noticed a striking contrast between the quest for excellence in each athlete and the lackluster business practices I had observed lately in many organizations. In contrast to the athletes giving every ounce of their skill and effort, it seemed many businesses were trying just to survive, not to thrive. Their efforts seemed focused more on how much cost they could reduce than on how much value they could create.

I wanted to write a book that would inspire world-class performance and challenge readers to examine and improve upon key areas in their work and personal lives. My hope was to inform, inspire, and leave a lasting impression that serves as a catalyst for action...a resurgence. Leaders seemed more focused on keeping their jobs than on doing their jobs. Businesses seemed more intent on holding than building. People were trying not to lose...their homes, their money, and their jobs. That's very different than trying to win! I decided to use the Olympics as a metaphorical springboard to remind readers that world-class performance, individually and collectively, is the only acceptable standard.

World-Class Performance tells a great comparative story of the presence or absence of leadership and its effect on the success or failure of an organization. This book reaffirms that all great institutions are built by leaders who demonstrate the bedrock values of integrity and trust.

In this book are stories of an imploding dynasty, a paragon of superior innovation, a model of exemplary execution and a strategy that sums up an era of dramatic change. I endeavored to tell big stories with verve and vigor.

The first person with whom I shared this idea was Ken Shelton, whom I have known for three decades. In the mid-1980s, we worked closely together for several years, crafting an award-winning approach to organization integration, executive and leadership development, and change management. He would go on to become a key writer for one of the best-selling books of all time (and one of my favorite books), the *7 Habits of Highly Effective People* authored by Stephen R. Covey. I had been an avid reader of Ken's magazines and newsletters for three decades. A prodigious achiever, his talents are impressive.

Ken Shelton was excited to join in and help. Ken and I believe these qualities will be the catalyst for the "blueprint for recovery" in these challenging and disorienting times. In the book, I use an Olympic theme to dispense advice to organizations and leaders at all levels about how to get back on the winning track. He has been a true advocate and coach in helping me navigate through the many challenges inherent in writing a book.

I want to thank those who have reviewed and provided numerous valuable suggestions to earlier drafts of this book; I note particularly the ideas flowing from David Allen, Ken Blanchard, Mike Stafford, Jim Belasco, Beverly Kaye, Dave Ulrich, Gifford Pinchot, Dan Burrus, Neil Novich and John Kotter. I am indebted to all for their support and insights.

The backing and support of my team, including Dave Sullivan, Sharon Doyle, Joe DiDonato, Cynder and Mark Niemela, and Eileen and John Foster, kept the lights on during dim periods. I am thankful for the re-entry of Suzanne Browning, my co-director from my McDonnell Douglas days in the mid-1980s, back into my life. Also lending vital support were Mort Topfer, former vice chairman of Dell and friend extraordinaire, and friends Mike and Mary Anne Morelli, Tony Coppola, Joe Cutcliffe, and Barry Leavitt. Special thanks go to Debbie McGrath for her generosity of spirit and to Adnan Saleem and Savitha Malar for their assistance.

To all the readers and kindred spirits who read and develop from these pages, my heartfelt thanks and best wishes to each one of you.

And finally, thanks and love to my children, Chelsie and David, for inspiring me to stretch to new heights during challenging times and their incredible patience with me as I tried to write a meaningful book. This book could not have been written without their love and amazing support. They are the greatest gifts in my life.

FOREWORD

By Ken Shelton, editor of *Leadership Excellence*

For most of my thirty-year tenure as editor of *Leadership Excellence* magazine, I have known Michael G. Winston, global head and chief organization and leadership strategy officer at Lockheed, McDonnell Douglas, Motorola, Merrill Lynch, and then Countrywide Financial.

And so I was pleased when Michael informed me that he was writing this book. Both of us have seen and experienced the good, the great, the bad, and the ugly in organizational performance. When you witness the rise and fall of leaders and organizations, as Michael and I have done over the decades, you learn lessons both in your head and heart. Perhaps nothing professionally is as gut-wrenching as seeing your company close its doors, lay off thousands of people, sell off assets, and leave many people with debt.

Leaders of failed enterprises own much of the blame for poor performance—even if they do their best to dodge it, as has Italian Captain Francesco Schettino of the wrecked cruise ship *Costa Concordia*, which grounded off the coast of Italy after sailing too close to shore, taking the lives of thirty-two passengers and crew. Captain Schettino was accused of several crimes (abandoning his ship, manslaughter, and causing the shipwreck). But now the master of the ill-fated ship says he's innocent and that the truth will be told—in his new book, of course. He says that he did all he could do to help—and he is sticking to his story that he tripped and fell into a lifeboat. Salvage operations continue at the site.

As eyewitnesses to such business wrecks and salvage operations—and derelict captains of various leader-ships—Michael and I care even more about competitiveness, performance, results, relationships, outcomes, and sustainability.

For inspiration in writing his book, Michael looked to the 2012 London Summer Olympic Games, where performance is everything (yes, even politics takes a back seat). After thirty years of editing *Leadership Excellence* magazine (some sixty-six hundred articles), I came to realize that organizations tend to have either a political or a performance culture.

I define politics broadly as any activity that diverts, distracts, delays, deters, or destroys value-added performance. One insight that I gained from working with Stephen R. Covey as his writer on *7 Habits of Highly Effective People* and *Principle-Centered Leadership* was this: most people have far more talent (performance potential) than their companies (political cultures) even allow them to use.

Few managers or leaders are pure politicians or pure performers. We are all composites, but the best of the breed have a bias for high performance and do all they can to ensure that their culture is all about excellent performance in the best interests of all stakeholders (a stock phrase in many corporate mission statements).

Why, then, are politics so prevalent? Why are so many firms more oriented to pervasive politics than peak performance?

In political cultures, the means to getting ahead include game-playing, positioning, politicking, parading, palavering, jockeying, backbiting, kissing up, flattering, stealing credit, and engaging in deceit, treachery, and even trench warfare.

Who tends to get ahead in political cultures? The tallest, toughest, biggest, loudest, brightest, most articulate, best dressed, most popular, physically endowed, financially flush, most talented, sociable, savvy, and smooth.

Once found out, corporate politicians can be very hard to ferret and flush out because their support structure and systems are sunk like roots into the soil of the culture. Indeed, they may well have the backing of the boss. And even if they lack support from the top, they may get applause from other folks, with whom they share the spoils. They also seek protection in legislation—in laws and regulations governing hiring, firing, promoting, electing, selecting, and admitting. They are experts at manipulating the internal recognition and reward system—often seeking and receiving various (but mostly meaningless) awards, honors, medals, badges, and certificates.

And so, once in charge, the politicians play a shell game whereby they keep all players guessing—and few winning. Meanwhile, they make out like bandits, having their hands in several cookie jars and their feet in the soothing spas of passive income streams. The result of all this political posturing can best be depicted as a gulf between what we really want and what we settle for. We deserve our fate if we blindly follow political leaders, especially if we are guilty of passive resistance, ignorance, activism, apathy, ambition, silence, aggression, sabotage, or sloth.

So, how do we turn political quagmires into performance cultures?

- Declare your area to be a performance environment—and then see that this declaration is translated into vision, mission, roles, and goals. Fight against rules and regulations that compromise your ability to create and maintain a performance environment.
- Set performance standards with people and hold them accountable to measurable or discernible performance objectives and standards.
- Eliminate double standards, sacred cows, political seed-beds, exclusive access, preferential treatment, and exceptions to the rules.
- Make an example of someone—fire a prominent executive who prizes politics over performance. The message will travel fast.
- Reward, promote, and recognize the real performers. Sing their praises. Prize their work.
- Make resources available to them.

Good luck. Replacing politics with performance, like ridding your lawn of weeds, is no small task. But the payoffs are immense. As Michael says, the stakes are high, and yet the rewards for world-class, Gold-medal performance excellence can be exponential.

INTRODUCTION

The business media is overwhelmed with books about companies that already get it and want to go from "good to great" or from "great to greater." These are the companies "in search of excellence," to quote authors and consultants Tom Peters and Bob Waterman. They are in relentless pursuit of perfection.

But what of the companies that haven't seen the light? And what of the employees feeling trapped in these companies, unable to leave? This book profiles a change strategy that works with leaders and organizations at both ends of the spectrum and offers a time-tested strategy for continuous improvement. When implemented properly, the workforce commits to becoming and remaining a force for change and exemplary performance.

Implementing a new strategy requires current and emerging leaders who can drive an organization, energize its operations, and inspire its people. This book was written for you…current and emerging leaders. It is for the select few who always step up, build a competitive edge, and differentiate themselves in clear and compelling ways. You know who you are. You are relentlessly pursuing greater accomplishment and impact.

This kind of leader personifies the organization's purpose through values, thinking, and character—all of which are necessary to inspire and energize

High-performance leaders and organizations believe that words and deeds should match. They have the guts and intestinal fortitude to keep their promises through thick and thin, in good times and bad.

commitment to the strategy and goals of the organization and secure the allegiances required to make any bold purpose succeed. Clearly, an essential element of leadership is trust.

High-performance leaders and organizations believe that words and deeds should match. They have the guts and intestinal fortitude to keep their promises through thick and thin, in good times and bad. It is in translating the commitment to consistent, purposeful action, often under fire (business downturn, budget crisis, etc.) that leadership is truly tested.

Without the requisite character and integrity, the organization is built to fail and will not last. According to the noted Edward R. Murrow:

To be persuasive, we must be believable;
To be believable, we must be credible;
To be credible, we must be truthful.

So many leaders of the recent past have failed themselves, their families, their shareholders, and their neighbors on the most important of leadership behaviors: honesty, integrity, and ethical decision-making. It is time to recognize and celebrate the leaders who exemplify these qualities. They are the true "game-changers."

High-performing organizations recruit talented individuals with these qualities and place them in focused, driven teams. They let their skills, drive, intelligence, and creativity rise to the surface. They train them, challenge them, and focus them on rewarding challenges and opportunities. They give them the place, space, knowledge, and opportunity to excel. By doing so, their talents can shine through, and the company develops another generation of leaders.

When I arrived at Motorola in the 1980s, I was amazed that a company like this actually existed—one that cared about its people; was full of great opportunity; was organized for speed, achievement, and agility; celebrated the achievements and milestones of its employees; and earned great loyalty from its people. Management was passionate about finding the right people.

Over my career, I have been uplifted by caring, kind, and compassionate leaders—qualities that are rare in competitive cultures. As I have now worked for the opposite type of leaders, I am even more committed to building cultures designed to nurture and empower people to treat each other well, work together, and BEAT their competitors! They do well by doing right.

The best leaders have a knack for seeing talent. They have a sense for who is the right fit for the company and who will succeed. They have a proven track record for bringing in the right talent and helping them develop. If they feel you have potential, they let you know of their strong belief in you, which enables people to believe in themselves. They have a way of leveling the playing field and helping everyone feel like they have a seat at the table. While they expect a lot from people, they also expect a lot of themselves.

NEW RULES, NEW NORMAL

This book covers the "new rules" used by great leaders and organizations during turbulent times to tap and leverage the talents and skills of those around them: stimulating high performance, sparking creativity and imagination, developing leaders, encouraging collaboration, and inspiring loyalty. This understanding is based upon nearly thirty years of experience serving as global head, worldwide organization and leadership strategy for several Fortune 100 companies.

Working across several business sectors (high technology, financial services, and aerospace) I partnered with C-suite officers, developing the business model, crafting strategy, creating culture, and selecting and developing leaders. I also provided strategic guidance to the CEO and executive team on business planning, execution, and human capital issues across the globe.

The most successful leaders develop and nurture champions, dramatize goals and direction, build skills and teams, and spread enthusiasm.

———

Through this experience, I have come to learn that the most successful leaders develop and nurture champions, dramatize goals and direction, build skills and teams, and spread irresistible enthusiasm. They encourage, teach, listen, facilitate, and even excite. Their actions are consistent. The focus of development is on continuous improvement and self-renewal.

It's time to advance and celebrate leadership at the highest level—leadership that is vision-driven and values-based. Let's encourage leadership that inspires, empowers, and pursues noble ends. I hope the ideas in this book ignite people. Perhaps we can prevent a reoccurrence of the leadership deficit we've recently experienced. High-performing leaders lift up shareholders, customers, employees, and society. A groundswell of support for these ideas might spur a transformation in business practices.

This is a book of many ideas. Some are new; some are not. The way they are put together is new.

CHAPTER 1

WORLD-CLASS COMPETITION

Adopt the Olympic motto: Citius, Altius, Fortius

The essence of the Olympics is embodied in its motto: "Faster. Higher. Stronger." This book was started in the wake of the 2012 Summer Games in London, showcasing performances by ten thousand athletes from around the world. As I put the finishing touches to this book, the Sochi Winter Olympics had ended months ago. The 2014 Olympic Winter Games marked the first time the Russian Federation had hosted the Winter Games since the break-up of the USSR. Ninety-eight events were held in fifteen sports, and over the two-plus weeks, more than three thousand athletes from around the world did their best to go faster, jump higher, and be stronger than their competitors. In the process, they made the impossible…possible.

The Olympics inspire us as do few other events in the world. The pageantry, the drama, the coming together of different people and cultures are a spectacle to behold. We learn a lot from these elite athletes and from the Games themselves.

We admire the Olympian's laser-like focus on winning. Some win Gold medals; others do not. But every one of them shows up prepared and ready, having spent the days, weeks, months, and years preceding the games focusing their energy on winning.

As we watch the Games, we learn the stories of struggle, sacrifice, and discipline. We rejoice in the victories and agonize at the defeats. We sit mesmerized as the athletes demonstrate the discipline, focus, and commitment necessary to win.

The Olympic Games compel us to want to achieve our own higher objectives. So how will you respond? What race are you running, and how will you begin or continue your journey to the Gold? Who will support you, and how will you remain committed to achieving your objectives? What will winning look like when you get there?

In today's fast-paced world, we are running a race every day—in our organizations and in our personal lives. Do you have the clarity, focus, and commitment to win? Can you rise to meet the 3C challenge? In a world of citius (faster), altius (higher) fortius (stronger)…

Are you fast enough to meet and beat your Competition?
Are you reaching high enough to delight your Customers?

Are you as strong as your Company needs you to be?

The race is on: are you fit to win? Remember those days when life was a little easier, when you could kind of predict the future, when you knew who the competition was and that the playing field was level? Well, those days are over. Life and business as usual…are unusual. Structural, permanent changes create new technologies, introduce new competitors, influence workforces, and alter attitudes in the marketplace. External events shape the future of any person, team, or organization. It's happening to everybody, every industry, every organization.

It is happening to you.

We live in an increasingly competitive and complex global business environment. It demands new strategies and tactics, sharper skills, and new ways of thinking about the big picture and the bottom line. The pace has never been so grueling; the stakes never so high. This environment taxes the best leaders and companies.

Academicians, researchers, consultants, and practitioners tell us that change is occurring at a blistering pace, leaving many people unprepared. True enough. Wave after wave of technological breakthroughs have revolutionized entire industries overnight. Wrenching political changes are bringing new opportunities and fresh risks. Competition in global markets is growing fiercer by the day. More sophisticated customers expect ever-higher levels of quality, customization, convenience, and timeliness.

Success today will not become success tomorrow without adapting strategy, style, and structure to an ever-changing environment. Rather than rest on our laurels, you and I must look ahead to the challenges of the future. Change cannot and will not be arrested. Organizations must change and adapt just to stay in the game.

The leaders who dominate in this new era will not only understand the changes affecting them, but they will seize them, master them, and use them to their advantage to achieve ever-higher performance. Every business is seeking to reengineer itself to adapt to a changing environment and seek a competitive edge in the global marketplace. So, too, must we.

What worked in the past no longer guarantees success today, let alone tomorrow and beyond. Experience is often not the best teacher. Conventional wisdom provides little guidance or comfort in a turbulent and radically redefined world, where business as usual is a sure prescription for failure.

New leadership is needed—leadership that goes against the grain, challenges conventional wisdom, and pushes the status quo.

Just before my writing on June 4, 2014, I watched a television interview in which Elon Musk, CEO of Tesla Motors, announced that all of his patents—once so zealously protected—were now open. "Tesla will not initiate patent lawsuits against anyone who, in good faith, wants to use our technology," he wrote in a blog post. Tesla's competitors can now freely take advantage of its batteries, chargers, or sunroofs.

His reasons for doing this are not entirely altruistic. Tesla makes electric cars and will only succeed if the entire electric vehicle industry succeeds. It needs other companies to help build charging stations, to improve batteries, and to change the perception that only rich people drive them. Tesla wins if its patents help Ford improve its batteries, which then leads Chrysler to make more electric vehicles, which then leads General Motors to start a chain of charging stations. If open patents can promote standardization, it would likely mean faster innovation for all. This is a clear example of breakthrough thinking.

Welcome to the new normal of change, uncharted territory, unprecedented challenges, and new realities on a daily, even hourly basis. Traditional ways of competing have reached a level of parity whereby businesses cannot distinguish themselves just on the basis of quality, technology, product, or price. Excellence in these areas is table stakes in today's global marketplace—the price of simply entering the game. Going to the next level—superior performance on each of these key dimensions—requires superior skill sets and strategies.

A major player in the financial services sector stated the following in its Annual Report a decade ago:

> *Our people have worked hard to reshape the company into one capable of performing at the highest level. We have built a solidly profitable and strategically sound platform on which we can grow for years to come... We are positioned to*

succeed in each of our businesses, responsibly and in a manner consistent with the uncompromising expectations of our clients and shareholders.

The rhetoric was great. However, the reality was somewhat less than the promise. Three years later, that same company—Merrill Lynch—was acquired for pennies on the dollar. While they had been independent for nearly one hundred years, they are now but a division of a much larger company. What was good enough then…is no longer good enough now.

This is a tale of two worlds. There is the one we have today: global economic crisis, concern about climate change, lack of trust in the corporate (and government) sector. Then there's the likely world of tomorrow: limited resources, stricter environmental regulation, and more transparency (hopefully) in the way business is done.

This new world will reward leaders and companies that innovate with sustainability in mind, allowing them and their customers to cut costs, find new markets, and recapture customers' trust. In short, it will reward inspired action with real results.

This challenge requires that we empower the leaders of today and tomorrow who are willing to turn ideas into action and then impact. These leaders have the sunny conviction necessary to carry the team through storms of biblical proportions.

THE COMING BUSINESS REVOLUTION

The system is about to change. It has to. To understand how, look to the innovative companies hard at work at their future…and ours. The system has grown impossibly expensive, bureaucratic, and inefficient. The new frontier is businesses that will cut costs by squeezing out inefficiencies and boosting communication and transparency, turning their world into a real, functioning marketplace.

Today's intense competition has eroded many traditional sources of competitive advantage. Technology can be copied, economies of scale and scope are less important, and a global business environment makes it tough to control access to resources or sales channels.

The ways in which people are managed and led, in contrast, can lead to competitive advantages that are much harder to imitate. Today, it is clear that human capital and intellect drives success and long-term competitive advantage. Recently, this was affirmed by 71 percent of CEOs surveyed, according to IBM Corporation in the August 12, 2013, issue of *Fortune* (p. 45).

That said, in many cases, the resources required to beat the competition in tomorrow's markets are beyond the capability of any individual company, leading to new entities and alliances. Increasing economic interdependence among industrialized countries, the growing needs of developing countries, and the disintegration of barriers to the flow of information, money, and technology are further accelerating the trend toward global market integration.

These unprecedented changes are forcing companies worldwide to reevaluate their marketing assumptions, further define and revise their management strategies, shift to higher value-added products and services, offer new, tailored services, and reposition themselves in the global market in order to capitalize on emerging business opportunities. Does this excite or frighten you? Are you fully prepared? Is your team fully prepared?

THE ESSENCE OF CHANGE

Change is the dominating reality of the business world. It feels as if we are moving from **bedrock** to **quicksand**. The galloping pace of change demands an unprecedented response from organizations. Rapidly evolving technology, diminishing natural resources, increasing global competition, and a more diverse workforce all require organizations to learn and change more and to do it faster in order to remain competitive. To survive and prosper, companies must adopt a way of managing that is based on their capacity to learn and change—consciously, continuously, and quickly.

The best way to achieve support for change is to secure not only the cooperation but also the participation of the people who will be accountable for carrying out necessary tasks. Those people must participate in developing the goals and plans designed to achieve them. Planning sessions in which both management and staff brainstorm and contribute are the best builders of shared purpose, understanding, and commitment.

Teamwork and change are best fostered when individuals, work units, and groups work creatively and effectively across functional and organizational boundaries together as a team in the pursuit of clearly understood, mutually supportive organizational objectives. At Motorola, we used this principle to reorganize the largest business unit with transparency and collaboration. The restructuring was credited as the catalyst for a major turnaround and return to profitability.

As involvement increases, people begin to feel greater ownership for the results of their work. They begin to believe in their own ability to contribute to the real work of the organization, to the thinking and decision-making that determine its success. Thus, in this particular Motorola reorganization, we involved all stakeholders in the re-design and consequently, they felt they more impacted the outcome. I co-chaired the Design Committee of this project. It was one of my best career experiences.

There is no such thing as too much emphasis on managing change. Resistance efforts can be skillful and sly, especially if people are not invited to participate broadly. Critical elements of change integration include communication plans, resistance and champion handling, a change laboratory, feedback loops and reward systems, and training at all stages.

More often than not, business leaders underestimate the difficulty of managing change as well as the expectations of key stakeholders and participants. Change objectives can be derailed by the lack of executive leadership and participation, overlooking revenue enhancement opportunities, insufficient focus on critical success factors, lack of a true understanding of the current state of affairs, failure to consider all the alternatives, lack of a process orientation, thinking too small, and underestimating change integration issues.

There are all essential conditions for successful change and strategies for minimizing resistance to change. Over the course of my career, I have interviewed thousands of employees at every level before, during, and after major transformation and polled them on the critical success factors to accelerate change. Critical ingredients for success include the following practices:

- Have a clear vision and strategy that people can embrace.
- Build success upon enduring strengths.
- Ruthlessly prioritize to be certain the greatest efforts and best resources are on the biggest opportunities.
- Act quickly and decisively to minimize disruption.
- Create the power of a big "organization" with the flexibility of a small one.
- Challenge every assumption.
- Treat diversity as the significant asset it is.
- Communicate clearly and often with all constituencies.

TRYING NOT TO LOSE IS DIFFERENT THAN TRYING TO WIN

The lingering recession of 2008 has taken quite a toll. Many companies are still in survival mode. They are trying to survive, not grow. The same is true of some executives. Trying not to lose is far different than trying to win. We must encourage them to again try to win with world-class performance.

It's time to lean forward and position your company for greatness and achieve world-class performance. Regain your Olympic-like competitive edge, rekindle your desire to compete and win. Place a premium on exemplary performance in all dimensions: quality, productivity, service, and value. Growth and innovation are not only possible but necessary during dark times. Here's a snapshot of the difference:

TRYING NOT TO LOSE	TRYING TO WIN
Hold	Build
Survive	Thrive
Divest	Invest
Pause	Pounce
Scarcity	Abundance
Wait	Anticipate
Reduce cost	Add value
Delay	Accelerate
Consent	Invent
Imitate	Innovate
Realistic goals	Stretch goals

Today's winning leader is not just here to weather the storm; they are here to completely change the game.

Today's winning leader is not just here to weather the storm; they are here to completely change the game. These leaders engage all people as active participants in delivering value creation, and this includes everyone at every level of the organization and customer base.

MEETING THE COMPETITIVE CHALLENGE

To survive and thrive in the new environment, companies are setting new standards for productivity, quality, and service. Business strategies are changing. Companies are revamping their cultures to reflect the new values, management styles, and ways of doing business.

Accordingly, development programs must be designed to grow leaders who think strategically and globally, advocate needed change, support teamwork and employee growth, and deal constructively with ambiguity and complexity. Leaders must accelerate the pace of change in thinking and action to create the most energizing mission, soundest strategies, strongest management talent, and most empowering culture.

World-class competition is the ultimate proving ground of people, teams, and organizations. Competition brings together exquisitely prepared men and women in a pressure-cooker atmosphere—each of them vying for victory. The line between success and failure is often razor thin…no more than a hundredth of a second or a few millimeters. The winners will be those who best prepare both physically and mentally and give the extra effort that leads to victory.

CHAPTER 2

MODEL THE OLYMPICS

Mirror the best models of performance

In our quest to win—to become a competitive high-performer, both as individuals and as teams/organizations—we might well seek to model the Olympians. Olympic-like performance standards provide a clarion call for business leaders to recognize anew that it is all about The Leading Edge: the commitment, pursuit, and achievement.

Olympians *always* go for greatness. Yet, too many companies today seem to be settling for survival. It is time to once again go for greatness, for world-class, the platinum standard.

Great examples of excellence in action can be found at the 2012 London Olympics in Usain Bolt, Jamaican sprinter and triple Gold medalist; Manteo Mitchell, the USA relay hero who broke his leg but kept running; Michael Phelps, the American swimmer who became the most decorated athlete in Olympic history; his Gold medal teammate Ryan Lochte; and the American women's gymnastics team.

Winning athletes are generally naturally gifted. For example, some of Ryan Lochte's physical gifts were bestowed upon him at birth through genetics: broad, flexible shoulders to power his strokes and hyper-extending knees to super-charge his kicks. But natural gifts (genetics) are only the starting point to world-class performance.

During the run-up to the Olympics, Lochte averaged forty miles of interval training in nine swim practices a week. Four days a week, Ryan's strength and conditioning coach, Matt Delancey, conducted grueling ninety-minute conditioning sessions. He created contraptions to make a hard job even harder. As a case in point, on most mornings, Lochte wore a belt connected by pulleys to a cable calibrated to fifty pounds of resistance, and as he swam laps, his coach increased the weight. How about you? Are you pushing yourself hard enough to build on your strengths?

STORIES OF OLYMPIC GREATNESS

Confucius said, "The will to win, the desire to succeed, the urge to reach your full potential—these are the keys that will unlock the door to personal excellence."

In the 2012 London Olympic Games, Michael Phelps swam like a porpoise and competed like a shark. He competed at four Olympics, from age fifteen to twenty-seven, and won twenty-two medals, including eighteen Gold medals. He was so good that when he won six medals—four of them Gold!—at the 2012 Olympics, it was simply expected.

Gabby Douglas leapt like a deer and flew like Peter Pan. In 2012, she was not even old enough to drive a car, but she was experienced, confident, and athletic enough to elevate her team to a Gold medal, win one for herself as the best gymnast in the world, and add to the twenty-nine Gold medals won by American women.

Manteo Mitchell was so driven to compete that he ran with a broken leg so his teammates could race for a medal another day. "Every step that I took was like Jell-O on my left leg," Mateo said while leaning on crutches the next day. "I don't know whether you can call it God or adrenaline or just the spirit of USA in my heart. I just didn't want to quit, and I just kept going."

Jamaican sprinter Usain Bolt ran like a cheetah and roared like a lion. Never had a human being been timed running so fast. He won three Gold medals at the 2008 Olympics, followed by three more in 2012.

There were equally talented athletes from all around the world. The global community was well-represented with brilliant accomplishment.

The essence of this incredible 2012 Olympic story and all others is that we all enter the world with the same Olympic possibilities, be they athletic or otherwise. We may experience disappointments and even crushing losses on our journey, but we must never lose our competitive spirit. Keep on pushing.

AMERICA'S CUP: STARS AND STRIPES

Perhaps you recall the exciting times when American yachtsman Dennis Connor skippered the *Stars and Stripes* to victory. Connor won the Bronze medal at the 1976 Olympics, two Star World Championships, and was a four-time America's Cup winner. The lessons of his wins are timeless.

I was reminded of this in 2006, when I attended the Milken Institute Global Conference as a presenter. It was an electrifying experience to meet and interact with the best minds in business, economics, politics, and entertainment all in one place. It was like the Academy Awards for everyone not in show business and is referred to as Davos West.

It was a thrill to be in the same place as Sumner Redstone, Terry Semel, Steve Wynn, Steve Forbes, Michael Milken, and T. Boone Pickens. The non-business group included Andre Agassi, Michael J. Fox, then-Sen. John Kerry, then-Gov. Arnold Schwarzenegger, William Bennett, and Kirk Douglas. One celebrated attendee was Ted Turner, rambunctious founder of CNN, Turner Broadcasting Network, and then-owner of the Atlanta Braves. While speaking to an audience of thousands, Mr. Turner commented on his role in the America's Cup and the fact that America, once a heralded competitor in this world-renown competition, is hardly ever mentioned anymore.

The America's Cup is the most famous and prestigious regatta in the sport of sailing. It is also the oldest active competition in international sport. It predates the modern Olympics by forty-five years. It is a challenge-driven yacht series that currently involves a best-of-nine series of match racing (a dual between two boats).

The trophy was held by the New York Yacht club from 1852 to 1983. Then the cup was won by the Australian challenger *Australia II*, ending the longest winning streak in the history of sports. The Australians recovered from a bad start to win the America's Cup 4–3 in a best-of-seven format. This victory broke the 132-year winning streak. One hundred thirty-two years!

Defeated skipper Dennis Conner won the Cup back four years later with the yacht named *Stars and Stripes*. He fended off an unprecedented thirteen challengers to do it. This victory rekindled interest in the sport—especially American interest.

There are significant lessons to be learned from the *Stars and Stripes* victory that are as relevant to captains of industry as are those of the Olympics. A common theme is triumph over hardship and adversity.

BUSINESS PARALLELS

There are clear parallels between Olympic and Olympic-like performances and high-performing business teams. In both, when the going gets

Challenge brings out the best in champions, whether the performance standard is athletic or business.

tough, the tough get going. Challenge brings out the best in champions, whether the performance standard is athletic or business. This tenacity is especially needed in an unsteady economy.

Every two years, we are amazed by the accomplishments and feats of Olympians from the world over. We are inspired by their performances as much as we are by their personal stories. Consider Switzerland's Dominique Gisin from the 2014 Sochi Winter Olympics.

Gisin won the Gold medal in women's downhill Alpine skiing. She shared the Gold with Tina Maze as they both completed their runs with the same exact time, a first in Olympic history in that event. This accomplishment is inspiring. However, when you factor in that Gisin had never won a medal before and that she had fought her way back from nine knee surgeries to compete, her performance is nothing short of amazing. Clearly, Ms. Gisin's dream was to compete at the highest level in the sport she loved, and she did everything it took to get there. And she won! Think about your career. How do you deal with adversity? When things get really tough, how do you respond?

Bruce Jenner is quite likely the world's most famous "World's Greatest Athlete." He owes his notoriety to several forces that came together and branched out from the two most important days of his life: July 29 and 30, 1976, when he won the Olympic Gold medal in the decathlon in Montreal.

Jenner's life combines a plethora of sports stories that have become almost clichés. He was the solitary, single-minded slave to training who forsook many creature comforts to prepare for his moment of glory. Dyslexic, he fit the classic redemptive mold—the athlete who struggled to overcome an ailment or hardship to achieve excellence. And he did struggle. From his tenth-place finish in the decathlon at the 1972 Games until the 1976 Olympics, he trained, on average, eight hours a day.

Bruce was 26 and looked like the classic all-American guy when he competed in the Montreal Games in the heat of the Cold War. Competing in the ten-event, track-and-field ordeal that traditionally crowns the "world's greatest athlete," he defeated defending champion Nikolai Avilov from the USSR, breaking his own world record with 8,618 points. He brought home a Gold medal in the year of America's Bicentennial. It doesn't get better than that.

Jenner's performance proves that breakthroughs are possible during headwinds as well as tailwinds. For example, three top technology powerhouses—HP, Polaroid, and Texas Instruments—all got their start in the 1930s, during the Great Depression. The recession of 1957 saw the invention of the semi-conductor. In the midst of "stagflation" of the 1970s, a small start-up named Microsoft was founded. So, too, did this occur in this era. The iPad, iPhone, Kindle, Flip, and Zipcar were all invented in a deep recession. So were Tesla and SpaceX. It can be done.

In business as on the field of athletic competition, we must play on our toes, not sit back on our heels. As famed coach Vince Lombardi said, "Winning isn't everything, but the will to win is everything."

In challenging times, companies get leaner, fitter, and more focused. You gain competitive advantage by ensuring a preemptive leadership position and stoking competitive vigor. As the environment becomes increasingly complex, executives are finding it more important to step back from day-to-day concerns to look at the broad range of issues, management tools, and processes that can make their organizations more productive, competitive, and profitable.

Many leaders, hungry for quick-fix solutions, gobble up the latest management theories, only to abandon them when hoped-for improvements do not occur immediately. As opposition and competition rise, more executives realize that strategic management of organizational change must be thoughtfully planned, carefully monitored, and consistently reinforced. Don't just survive…thrive. How are you doing by this standard?

THE PAST IS NOT PROLOGUE

Since success can breed failure, never get complacent. *The Wall Street Journal* once published a series of advertisements from a leading consulting firm. The titles are provocative: "The more money your company makes, the more likely it is to lose money." "Discontent—the most valuable management asset, the most difficult to keep." "The longer a business operates, the less efficient it becomes—particularly if it is successful and profitable." In short, nothing fails like success! Stay hungry!

Change can be disruptive, dynamic, pervasive, and fast. Organizations face the reality that change will test their strategies, operations, and structures. They must adapt and change just to stay in the game. To survive, to excel, to win the game, organizations must seek the perspective, tools, and expertise to meet the challenge of change head-on.

The pace and complexity of change are likely to increase in the years ahead. No organization can be sure of a secure future. Scientific and technological developments can transform the very ground on which organizations learned to operate. Geopolitical scales may shift. Changes can come from "out of the blue." Traditional competencies or market niches can be challenged by new technologies, new skills, and new products.

Slumbering giants can be shaken to life and left staring at new competitors who have new ideas and approaches. Many organizations with a long history of success have failed because they refused to accept change as a fact of life. Recent casualties include Sharper Image, Netflix, J.C. Penney, and Hostess. *The Washington Post* was recently acquired by Amazon's founder Jeff Bezos. There will be many more "out-of-the-box" business moves. This is a time of "survival of the fittest." Are you fit? How can you build even further on your strengths?

We can consent to what happens to us; *resent* what happens to us; or *invent* what happens to us!

Today's success does not guarantee tomorrow's. Experience is an adequate guide only when changes are made in small increments. When decisions are strategic and have sweeping, irreversible consequences, intuitive and experience-based action can be grossly inadequate. Successful performance in the uncharted waters of the future requires executives to be open to new ideas, to challenge past assumptions, to question conventional wisdom, and to engage in healthy introspection.

We have three choices: we can consent to what happens to us; resent what happens to us; or *invent* what happens to us! Successful individuals and companies invent what happens to them. They invent their future. They constantly innovate, seek self-renewal, and target improvement after improvement, percent by percent, discipline by discipline. Corporate winners explore and master powerful strategies for identifying, under-standing, and stimulating the vision and day-to-day actions necessary to enhance customer service, productivity, and innovation. What are you doing to invent what happens to you, your team, and your company?

CHAPTER 3

CREATE A COMPELLING VISION

Watch the horizon, not the wake

Michael Phelps was driven to be the first Olympian in history to win eight Gold medals in a single Olympic Games. He had prepared for this since he was a young boy. In the 2008 Beijing Games, he had already won six of his eight Gold medals when he found himself in a most unusual situation. He was well behind the leader in his seventh race, the 100-meter fly...

Artist and entrepreneur Erik Wahl tells how "back in November 2007 (less than nine months before the summer Olympics in Beijing), Phelps slipped and fell outside of his training facility in Ann Arbor, Michigan. Sadly, he broke his wrist. The media quickly seized upon the trauma and drama of the situation and wondered how long this would keep Michael out of the water. Medical pundits speculated on how badly this would affect Michael's training protocol. They asked if he would even be able to compete in the Olympic Games at all."

But Phelps thrives on adversity. He had a vision, and he planned to realize it. Nothing would deter him. He got back in the water just days after breaking his wrist. With renewed enthusiasm, he designed a kickboard to support his surgically repaired wrist and propelled himself back and forth across the pool over and over without the use of his arms at all. This method of training was to become his "new normal."

Wahl continues, "Nine months later, during the 100-meter fly in the Beijing Olympic Games, Michael's quest for his seventh Gold medal was falling short. With less than one lap to go, Michael was nearly a half body length behind Serbian swimmer Milorod Cavic, a seemingly insurmountable challenge. All of a sudden, the crowd began to cheer and stomp its feet. Michael surged forward, turning on the gas and dropping into his extra gear. He used the strength of his powerful new kick to finish first and win the Gold by 1 / 100TH of a second. Olympic viewers around the world were stunned.

"After the race, Bob Bowman, Michael's longtime coach confirmed that had it not been for Michael's broken wrist, a tremendous setback, Michael would not have won that race. Michael had won many championships with the sleekness of his long and powerful upper body. But the injury forced Michael to train differently and not rely on his greatest strength but rather to focus on the weakness of his legs."

Michael went on to achieve his goal of eight Gold medals in Beijing. In doing so, he broke iconic swimmer Mark Spitz's thirty-six-year-old record of seven Gold medals in one Olympics.

The best way to predict the future is to invent it.

So, too, it is in business. You can't guide a ship by watching the wake. The best way to predict the future is to invent it. High-performing leaders create and communicate a compelling vision of excellence. They know that true motivation for change comes from a desired "ideal," a vision of what is possible as a result of the change. They attract and energize their people by stating the vision and demonstrating the will and determination to see that the course is maintained.

People perform best when they unite with a keen sense of the vision—knowing where they are headed and that it is someplace special. If the vision is clear and compelling, it draws people together and pulls them forward. When Mark Zuckerberg explains the purpose of Facebook, he can energize his base by stating their purpose: "Our mission is to make the world more open and connected. We do this by giving people the power to share whatever they want and be connected to whoever they want, no matter where they are." Clear, compelling, and worthwhile.

The November 4, 2014, *Harvard Business Review* notes the evolving challenge of motivating talent in an article written by U.S. Chairman and Senior Partner of PwC Bob Moritz. He recalled that when he was moving through the ranks, he and his peers knew what they were doing, but did not ask why they were doing it. Generally, people from the Boomer generation did not give as much thought to their, or the firm's, role in society then as people do now. Today, Millennials everywhere don't only demand to know the organization's purpose—its reason for being—but are prepared to leave the firm if that purpose doesn't align with their own values. This point crystallizes the generational issues that many organizations are facing as they hire greater numbers of Millennials.

The vision must move the group's attention from the "now" to the inspiration of "what could be." People must have a purpose if they are to move purposefully. Without one, individuals drift, go their separate ways, and lose sight of the logic behind collective effort. Moreover, they must be energized by this purpose.

To win, today's executives must not only anticipate change, but shape it. This requires anticipation, vision, and managing from the future. Evolving from a small regional airline to one of the world's most respected brands in 2013, Singapore Airlines credits its vision to lead as a key to its current success. It is what enabled British Airlines to go from bloody awful to bloody awesome—the world's favorite as of a decade ago. It is what powered Bill Gates' vision of a "computer in every home" and the late Steve Jobs' inspiration of a "computer in every pocket, purse, dorm room, and bedroom." Vision enabled Ted Turner to transform broadcast news from what *has* happened to what *is* happening and enabled the creation of CNN.

Interestingly, the launch of CNN met with lukewarm reaction. In 1980, Turner sold one of his stations, WRET, for $20 million to help finance the launch of a twenty-four-hour live-news network called Cable News Network, or CNN. This was the first network to broadcast nonstop news coverage. Their niche was the breaking story. Journalists and investors mocked CNN, calling it "Turner's folly." They were wrong. In the late 1980s, profit and stature ended the ridicule—CNN earned praise for its coverage of several important events, including the explosion of the space shuttle *Challenger*, the 1989 San Francisco earthquake, and the Persian Gulf War. CNN was a very balanced news network as well, not swaying liberal or conservative ideologies. CNN's lack of pizzazz contributed to its reputation for straight, balanced journalism. Rather than television stations like ABC, NBC, and CBS, where the news anchors and correspondents were treated as stars, at CNN the news itself was treated as the most important part. Turner had a clear vision and executed a focused strategy to realize it.

A clear vision enables the organization to move quickly in the desired direction. Google founders Sergey Brin and Larry Page once walked into a venture-capital firm and were able to express their company's vision in one sentence: "Google provides access to the world's information in one click." Strategy, structure, systems, and processes all flowed from that one statement. Needless to say, they got their funding. A venture capital head once told me that if an entrepreneur could not articulate his vision in ten words or fewer, he wouldn't fund him/her a dime.

The vision must provide direction and definition, focus for structure and consistency, communicate the need for change, and instill enthusiasm, commitment, and pride. Once the initial vision is formulated, it becomes a standard against which decisions can be weighed and progress can be evaluated. The vision should create the thrust for all organizational activity, sharpening the focus so allocation of time, talent, and money and day-to-day decisions and direction are more easily rationalized, communicated, and understood. As President John F. Kennedy's "Man on the moon by the end of the decade" served as a rallying cry for a nation during the 1960s and beyond, so, too, could "Energy independence within ten years" serve to galvanize a country and focus collective efforts.

TO DO OR NOT TO DO?

Just as your vision defines which opportunities will be pursued, your vision also defines which opportunities will *not* be pursued. There is a wide range of opportunities for future business development facing every organization. No organization can pursue all future development options simultaneously. If it does, scarce resources become dissipated, as do the energy and creativity of those involved. Focus is lost, and with it goes the discipline to achieve the vision.

In my experience, many companies get the first part right and the second part wrong. They are clear on which opportunities to pursue. However, they do not clearly delineate the criteria that define which opportunities will not be pursued.

The most important role of a leader is to provide clarity. This is especially true about priorities. Are you clear on what is most important? Are your people clear on it? All leaders need to establish a strong sense of direction; address the key issues and opportunities they face; develop a common vision of what needs to be done and a viable plan to do it; and accelerate the heartbeat and pulse rate to make the right things happen faster.

The absence of a vision and strategic priority-setting process is, in my view, the single largest barrier to success. Activities and efforts are inconsistent and lack focus. Companies stumble from crisis to crisis. Excessive short-term orientation coupled with constrained thinking undermines focus on vision. Leaders must clearly delineate strategic priorities. Know what to say yes to and what to say no to. It matters.

Point your management team toward a navigational north star, and then communicate it broadly and deeply. Teams need to know where they are going. If the aiming point is clear, and the vision is compelling, it draws people together and pulls them forward.

Communication is key. Often a strategy falters because it's not understood. Ensure that the vision, mission, objectives, processes, and activities are clearly and fully communicated. Once you clearly communicate your vision, the team must spread the word. Communication can be formal or informal, ranging from one-to-one to large group meetings. In every situation, actions, behavior, and language (verbal and nonverbal) must communicate and symbolize the vision. These communications can secure enthusiastic commitment and contribute to strategic change.

Behavior is the most important form of communication. The vision-driven executives who model desired behaviors become agents of change. Such leaders are unswerving, uncompromising, and relentless in pursuing excellence.

A crystal-clear vision of the mission and objectives, along with shared purpose and clear goals, acts as a steering mechanism. Without well-focused goals, the organization and its members are adrift. With no focus on the future, people can only focus on the past and present. They must instead focus on present *and future* opportunities. Attract and energize people by painting an exciting vision of the future, motivating them by identification with a vision rather than with rewards and punishments. Vision and mission should guide day-to-day decision-making.

True motivation for change comes from some desired objective—a vision of what is possible as a result of the change. Developing a vision statement is an important process for both the leaders of the change and those who will most be affected by it. The mission and vision describe the outcome as well as the purpose underlying the change. Management must paint a simple, clear, and compelling vision with which people can identify. Where will you be in five years? What will your organization look like in ten years? Do your people know? Are you doing things now that will get you there?

Organizations having a clear vision, mission, and goals excel for four reasons:

1. The vision clarifies the nature and direction of the business, what it aspires to be, and where it is going. It dissipates the fog of

drift, opportunism, and management by crisis, replacing it with purposeful, goal-directed management.

2. It effectively channels action to where it is most effective in gaining the desired results.

3. It builds morale and the will to achieve.

4. It accelerates growth and achievement by kindling a strong desire to achieve planned objectives.

To ensure the vision is clear and focused, ask and answer these key questions: What is the thrust or focus for future business development? What is the scope of products, services, and markets that will and will not be considered?

With a clearly defined product and market scope, you have roped off the limits of the organization's future product and market efforts. But how much time and attention should be paid to the various products and markets within the scope? These products and markets include both current offerings and those new opportunities on the drawing board for the future (the strategic nursery). Priorities must be set so resources can be focused on implementing the organization's vision.

What key capabilities are required to make the vision happen? Every organization has capabilities—such as production, distribution, marketing, and sales—that are devoted to operations. The shape of the vision in terms of its impact on business development, product and market scope, and emphasis may well require human and physical resources that are new and different from those required by current operations. Will you develop or acquire them where there is no immediate operational pressure to do so? World class organizations and leaders do.

The vision must serve to rationalize allocation of strategic resources. Explore these strategic questions with your team:

1. What trends and assumptions should you consider in the world around you: political, regulatory, social, economic, and technological?
2. Are you considering them?
3. What trends or changes do you expect in the needs of your customers?
4. What trends or changes will affect your customer base?
5. What might happen that would reduce or increase the need for your product or service?
6. What trends or changes threaten or bolster your competitive advantages?
7. What trends or changes do you expect in your competition?
8. What do you expect your competitors to do?
9. Where might new competition come from?
10. What should we do about the above?

People who got it right include the late Robert Galvin, former Chairman and CEO of Motorola; Amazon's Jeff Bezos; Indra Nooyi, Chairman and Chief Executive Officer of PepsiCo.; Ford Motor Company's Alan Mulally;

the late Sanford McDonnell, former Chairman and Chief Executive Officer of McDonnell Douglas; and Mort Topfer, former Vice Chairman of the Board of Dell, Inc. Many others did as well.

They are distinguished because each had the courage to set the course and stay the course. They carefully considered the appropriate direction, then exercised the courage of their convictions not to bend with the wind when naysayers suggested an easier, usually more business-as-usual course. Deciding on the direction is like setting a strategic compass. There may be different routes, but the destination must remain clear so allocation of time, talent, and money and decisions and direction are more easily communicated and understood.

The best leaders move swiftly in support of their business vision, shedding businesses that deflect attention from the core businesses. While others talk a good game about exiting non-strategic or poorly performing businesses and product lines, the best leaders actually do it! They are clear on the scope of products and markets that will and won't be pursued.

They come to grips with the key issues and opportunities they face; they develop a common vision of what needs to be done and a viable plan to do it; and they accelerate the organizational pulse to make the right things happen faster. You can do this.

CHAPTER 4

SETTING STRATEGY

Define the pathway to high-performance

Strategy is the act of plotting the path to goal accomplishment. This begins with the process of describing key aspects and activities in the future (a vision) and developing a strategy for getting there. This activity must satisfy two criteria: desirability and feasibility. Desirability means the needs of the constituencies that support the business, and feasibility means there is a sensible strategy for getting there.

Consider these issues: Is there long-range direction for your product, technology, and customers? Is the strategy supportive of the purpose? Are your people knowledgeable and supportive about the business strategy? To what extent does the organization have clear goals? To what extent does the organization have defined plans to meet its goals? Do the goals support the purpose and strategy? Are they mutually developed and challenging, but also achievable?

Are they specific and measurable in time and results? Are goals universally understood?

High performers focus on opportunities and attract and energize people by painting an exciting future, and then motivating them with a mission rather than with rewards and punishments. They create something new out of something old.

While maintaining a strong presence in key markets, you might: 1) conduct detailed reviews of each business to determine its appropriate size for the expected market environment; 2) identify businesses where margins and growth prospects are lower, narrowing in on areas of sustainable competitive advantage; 3) carve out opportunities to increase productivity and earnings through improved allocation of resources; and 4) focus on what you do and how you do it.

Note the difference between today's strategic forces and those for the future. What opportunities to take advantage of your current competitive strengths might emerge from the anticipated trends and changes? What opportunities might emerge from your vision, which, though not directly related to current strengths, merit further assessment?

Manage your businesses as a portfolio. A wide range of opportunities confront your organization…deeper penetration of current markets with existing or improved products; expanding to new markets with current or improved products; developing or acquiring new products

Market leadership demands that you place bets—big ones and small. Deciding where to place those bets is the challenge.

for current markets; and developing new products for new markets. Market leadership demands that you place bets—big ones and small. Deciding where to place those bets is the challenge. Where do you put your talent? Where do you put your financial and other resources? What project should people work on? How much money should you allow them to spend? A significant number of ideas—none of them sure bets—contend for a finite supply of investment dollars.

Each project team clamors for attention and makes a compelling case, but no company can fund every idea—or even every project it undertakes. The organization cannot pursue all future development options simultaneously. If it does, scarce resources become dissipated, as do the energy and creativity of those involved. Focus is lost, and with it the discipline to achieve the vision. This can be costly. We have all seen this.

Increase capital allocation to those areas of the business that are key to achieving financial objectives. Decrease capital allocation to those areas that do not and will not provide consistently acceptable returns. Develop a process to coolly, rationally, and fairly reassess your businesses—business by business—and exit those that do not provide competitive advantage.

If not using scenario planning, please consider it. Scenario planning helps you anticipate and prepare for change—and thus gain competitive advantage. Traditional forecasting techniques often fail to predict big changes, especially when they are rapid and turbulent. Key opportunities and serious threats may be overlooked, putting the firm at risk. Scenario planning is designed to deal with major, uncertain shifts.

When it comes to long-range planning, many professionals freeze in their tracks. How can you plan beyond the next six months to a year when the future is full of uncertainties and unknowns? While no one can predict exactly how your business, industry, customers, suppliers, and operating environment will change over the next three to five years, it's important to prepare.

Scenario planning has its roots in military strategy studies. Herman Kahn was an early founder of scenario planning in his work related to nuclear war (thinking the unthinkable). Scenario planning was transformed into a business tool in the late 1960s and early 1970s, most notably by Pierre Wack, who developed the scenario planning system used by Royal Dutch/Shell. As a result of its use, Shell was prepared to deal with the late 1973 oil crisis and greatly improved its competitive position during the crisis and the oil glut that followed. The corporate world continued to embrace scenario planning throughout the 1980s and 1990s.

While no longer all the rage, it still works. Scenario planning isn't about predicting the future, but describing what's possible. The result of a scenario analysis is a group of distinct futures, all of which are plausible. The challenge then is preparing to deal with each of the possible scenarios.

Scenario planning helps business leaders identify the range of possible futures and their implications; what the company would need to do to be successful under each scenario; and their strategic options. By generating and evaluating strategic options, they are better prepared for the future, however it unfolds. While many companies use scenario planning in strategic planning, you can use this approach to generate insights and actions, rather than reacting to change as it occurs.

In my career, I've conducted scores of scenario planning sessions. Participants emerge engaged, clear, and confident in the options available to them. These sessions often take place in a setting of executives, technical experts, and industry leaders. Bring together a wide range of perspectives to consider scenarios beyond the widely accepted forecasts.

The scenario development process should include interviews with those managers who later will formulate and implement strategies based on the scenario analysis. Without their input, the scenarios may leave out critical details and may not lead to action if they do not address the issues important to those who will implement the strategy. In doing this, decision-makers can better recognize a scenario in its early stages, should it be the one that unfolds. Further, managers can better understand the source of differences of opinion that often occur when they are envisioning different scenarios without realizing it.

Managers will not take scenarios seriously if they deviate too much from their preconceived view of the world. Many prefer to rely on forecasts and their judgment, even if they miss important changes. To overcome this reluctance to broaden their thinking, create phantom scenarios that show the adverse results if the firm bases its decisions on the mainstream view when the reality turns out to be quite different.

Why do some companies reinvent competition in their markets while others seem unaware of the changing world? Successful teams—market leaders—excel at delivering a primary type of value to their chosen customers. The key is focus. Market leaders tend to choose a primary value discipline—best total cost, product, or total solution—and then build around it. Choosing a primary discipline to master means that a company stakes its reputation—and focuses its energy and assets—on a primary discipline to achieve success over time. Don't try to be all things to all people. As Peter Drucker advised: "Focus scarce resources on the greatest opportunities." Place your bets. Most importantly, remember that an elegant strategy is meaningless without the ability to execute flawlessly.

Concurrent with holding corporate positions, I was fortunate to teach at many executive programs around the world. An absence of a scenario planning mind-set is evidenced in the following true story, which occurred midway through my sixteen-year run (five weeks each year) as visiting professor in the Young Executive Program at Stichting de Baak in Noordwijk, The Netherlands. De Baak is in a beautiful location on the dunes overlooking the North Sea. One particular program was attended by about forty high-potential executives in large, Dutch family-run businesses. They were all "heirs to the throne." I had just come to Holland from Beijing and Shanghai and was describing the progress realized since my last visit to mainland China. A Dutch program participant asked why I was telling them about societal change in China and its increasing competitiveness. He told me that he had no aspirations to grow in China. I replied that his disinterest in China did not mean the Chinese had no interest in Holland. He explained his family had owned their business for nearly eighty years; it had always been Dutch-held and would always remain so. We discussed the changes prompted by globalization. He remained unconvinced.

Three years later, his company was bought by…you guessed it, a Chinese company.

CHAPTER 5

EXPECT GREAT RESULTS

Better to aim high and miss

Is "good enough" good enough? World-class athletic competition requires years of training to qualify for an event that can be over in seconds. One false move, one lapse in concentration, one fraction of a second can stand between quiet anonymity and a place in the record books. Facing a hundred ways to lose, give it everything you've got, pushing yourself to the limit and beyond.

Pushing himself to the limit and pulling away from the pack with every long stride, Olympic champion Usain Bolt crossed the finish line and waved his index finger in the 2012 Summer Olympics. He's still number one in the 100-meter dash. Maybe not better than ever, but Bolt is definitely back.

Only sixth-fastest of the eight runners at the halfway point a few nights prior, Bolt erased that deficit and overtook a strong field of competitors to win in 9.63 seconds, an Olympic record that let him join Carl Lewis as the only men with consecutive Gold medals in the marquee track-and-field event at the Summer Games.

At Beijing four years before, Bolt electrified the track and field world, winning Gold medals in world-record times in the 100 meters, 200, and 4x100 meter relay—something no man had ever done at an Olympics. His 100-meter record of 9.69, the one that came despite slowing down for celebratory chest-slapping at the finish line, only lasted until the next year's world championships, when he lowered the record to 9.58.

But the World's Fastest Man had been something less than Boltesque since then, in part due to several minor injuries to his back and legs. In 2010, he lost to Tyson Gay, the American who's a past world champion. A false start eliminated Bolt from the 100-meter race at the 2011 world championships, creating an opening for Yohan Blake. Then Bolt lost to Blake in the 100 and 200 at the Jamaican Olympic trials. This got Bolt's attention and kicked him into high gear.

In London, he took a while to get up to top speed, but once he found his extra gear, he left his world-class competitors in the dust. Once he found himself even with the leaders with about fifty meters left, Bolt did what he does best, even leaning in at the finish for good measure.

There's walking. There's running. And there's BOLTING! On the day described, Bolt had what it takes. One day his best will not be good enough. As the saying goes, "Staying #1 is infinitely harder than becoming #1." It is hard to get there. It is harder to stay there. (An actual bolt of lightning struck just after Bolt won the 100-meter title at the IAAF world championships in Moscow, on August 11, 2013.)

Is "good enough" good enough? Not if your competitor's product or service is better. In today's competitive environment, excellence is the only standard. If you are excellent, but so are your competitors…then you are only average. There is simply no way to differentiate your firm. You must find a way to stand out.

Key premises described long ago in Adrian Slywotzky's *Value Migration* are truer today:

- Companies cannot raise prices to cover higher costs. They must lower costs to accommodate rising customer expectations.
- Companies must aim for exemplary service. Their customers enjoy effortless, flawless, and instantaneous performance from one industry and want it from every other.
- Customers cannot compromise on quality and product capabilities. They must build products that deliver superior, flawless quality and eye-popping innovation.

The competition, complexity, and challenge today are extreme. This will not diminish. Thus, excellence is the price of admission to this high-stakes competitive business world. Flawless performance rules! To build and sustain a competitive advantage, companies must be excellent and unique.

Is "good enough" good enough? Not if your competitor's product is better. Even 99.9 percent right still leaves plenty of room for errors in today's complex world. For example: If banks were 99.9 percent right, twenty-two thousand checks would be deducted from the wrong bank accounts each hour. If surgeons were 99.9 percent right, five hundred incorrect surgical procedures would be performed each day. If druggists were 99.9 percent right, twenty thousand incorrect prescriptions would be processed each year. If airline pilots were 99.9 percent right, 730 unsafe landings would scare passengers flying into Chicago's O'Hare Airport each year. If 99.9 percent were good enough, two million documents would be lost by the IRS this year; twelve babies would be delivered to the wrong parents each day; 1,314 phone calls would be misplaced every minute.; 2,488,200 magazines would be published with the wrong covers; and 5,517,200 cases of soft drinks would be produced without any carbonation.

Interestingly, these statistics were from research done well over a decade ago, using then-current numbers and for the United States alone. Just imagine what those numbers would be today!

Nope, good enough is **not** good enough. The relentless pursuit of perfection is now a business imperative. These days, it is common to see an intense focus on excellence in product and service design and delivery. Goals abound for Six Sigma quality and lean manufacturing. I

It is better to aim high and miss than to aim low and hit.

---

was fortunate to be part of the inception of this movement. In late 1986, Bill Smith, a senior engineer and scientist at Motorola, introduced the concept of Six Sigma to up the company's game in quality and standardize the way defects were counted. To achieve Six Sigma, a process must not produce more than 3.4 defects per million opportunities. A Six Sigma defect is defined as anything outside of customer specifications.

I joined Motorola in early 1988. America had lost its competitive edge to the Japanese in industry after industry. In 1987, Bob Galvin, Chairman of the Board of Motorola, had just announced the company's commitment to a then-new initiative: Six Sigma. He saw this as a way to restore his company to prominence. Motorola was going to make quality its competitive edge. It was an amazing goal…committing to no more than 3.4 defects per million, better than 99.9 percent performance. The then-current defect rate was thirty-four thousand per million.

Mr. Galvin was asked if he was concerned that the goal was too high. Conventional wisdom suggests that for maximum motivational impact, a goal should be 50 percent achievable. Any higher and the goal is too easy. Any lower and the goal is increasingly out of reach, and motivation can plummet.

Conventional wisdom notwithstanding, Galvin said, "It is better to aim high and miss than to aim low and hit." Whether he is or is not the originator of that phrase is not the point. The point is that this principle became embedded in the DNA of an entire company of nearly 150,000 employees.

I served as co-chairman of one of the original Six Sigma implementation teams. The way the company institutionalized Six Sigma as a way of life was nothing short of magical, enabling Motorola to become the first company to win the Malcolm Baldrige National Quality award as a company in 1988. This award is given by the United States Congress. In describing Motorola's total transformation, one of the Malcolm Baldrige auditors noted that no matter where he went throughout Motorola's far-flung empire, every Motorolan with whom he spoke clearly understood and precisely articulated the vision, strategy, objectives, and processes of Six Sigma.

Six Sigma began as a methodology for enhancing product quality and became a catalyst for the movement on continuous improvement in every discipline. After implementing Six Sigma, Motorola used "learning-action-feedback" processes throughout the corporation to accelerate the pace of change. The process moved quickly into the business units through the development of Total Customer Satisfaction (TCS) teams, which worked within and across the businesses and the corporation.

Jack Welch, former President and CEO of General Electric, said, "A thing I have learned is the value of stretching the organization by setting the bar higher than people think they can go. Invariably, people find the way to get there, or most of the way. They dream and reach and stretch. The trick is not to punish those who fall short. If they improve, you reward them—even if they have not reached the goal. But unless you set the bar high enough, you'll never find out what people can do." Mr. Welch was also a passionate proponent of Six Sigma processes.

I believe that if you do not demand something out of the ordinary, you will get ordinary results. That is the rationale for stretch targets, which require big, athletic leaps of progress on measures like inventory turns, product development time, and manufacturing cycles. Imposing such imperatives compels companies to reinvent the way they conceive, make, and distribute products. So please ask yourself this question: Is it better to aim high and miss or to aim low and hit? Shouldn't you be aiming higher?

CHAPTER 6

ORGANIZE BY DESIGN, NOT DEFAULT

Organize for strength with speed

The uncertain global economy, coupled with geopolitical insta-bility and extreme competition, mandates that each business: sharply focus financial and management resources on highest return businesses; ruthlessly prioritize to be sure the greatest efforts are employed on the biggest opportunities; and build success upon key functional strengths.

Put the power of the entire organization (human, financial, technical, reputational, and physical resources) behind a few very big initiatives—ones that really count. Organize for strength with speed. One cannot overestimate the role organizational structure plays in facilitating certain kinds of behavior and restricting others. If you can transform this vision into action, you will up your game exponentially.

The responsibility of management is to make sure the goals and objectives of the organization are accomplished and that everyone understands what to do and why. Organization is a tool that, if used properly, enables you to accomplish goals more efficiently and effectively.

An organization structure in and of itself produces nothing. The structure, however, can *facilitate certain kinds* of behavior, while *restricting* other kinds of behavior. Thus, the structure can make it easier for some things to happen…while making it difficult, if not impossible, for other things to happen.

Some assumptions that influence the thinking about structure are myths. These include the notion that:

1. There is a structure that is right for each business, if we could only discover it.
2. If the right structure were in place, we wouldn't need to keep making all these changes.
3. There is a set of rational rules that should enable us to create this right structure.

These myths frustrate people and cause them to feel as if they can never catch up.

Research and experience confirm that no matter what structure is put into place, it will soon be out of date because the rate of change forces distortions in that structure. Changes in structure are often accomplished by the informal organization well in advance of formal structural changes.

If the formal structure lags too far behind real needs, people will work around the obstacles imposed by the formal structure. That said, some structures are better suited to certain phases of an organization than are others.

As any organization grows and becomes decentralized, silos appear, with similar functions doing similar work. During periods of significant revenue growth, these structures enable close-to-the-customer focus and responsiveness. When the market contracts, these duplicative functions are no longer affordable. In the current and projected economy, the organization must reduce or eliminate overlapping or redundant functions. Every organization structure should serve to strengthen focus, leverage, and synergy.

An effective structure supports the business objectives of quality with speed to market. It clearly defines and clarifies roles and responsibilities, fosters clear accountability, promotes efficiency, and minimizes duplication of effort. It should also eliminate functional and organizational barriers, facilitate timely communication and decision-making, and leverage distinctive competencies.

The organization structure should flow from the vision and strategy. The structure provides direction for achieving strategic, administrative, and operational plans. The structure provides the framework, facilitating certain kinds of behavior, and restricting or preventing other kinds of behavior.

A significant roadblock to enhancing bottom-line performance is a bloated structure. An inspiring vision and heavy capital investment are quickly offset if execution must occur in an organization with too many layers. Excessive layers impact decision-making, communication, cycle-time, and resource allocation.

The jobs and structures in any business must also be designed to support both operational processes and flexibility. Fragmented structures are the enemy of change. People performing narrow, repetitive tasks typically have little understanding of the context of their work or the results of the business processes in which they participate—better that jobs have broad scope, multiple tasks, integrative responsibilities, and clear lines of sight to the results of their work.

The best organizations continuously assess management practices to determine what makes the difference between success and failure. Organizational excellence is enhanced by aligning strategy, technology, processes, and people (in addition to structure) to support the business vision and success differentiators. Here are a few guidelines:

Designate the design criteria, principles, or objectives the design must address. If you repeatedly change your structure—decentralizing and then recentralizing; organizing by technologies and then by client groupings—you'll find that reorganization is highly disruptive and expensive, and often the new organization performs no better. Continual reorganization is a symptom of the lack of a model that guides changes over time.

Do not reward empire building. Reward efficiency instead. A healthy structure and culture eliminate all incentives to empire building. Titles and status tend to go to those with the most resources. A significant amount of political maneuvering is motivated by self-protection during meetings. Willingness to change is partly a function of perceptions of personal payoffs. So reward new behaviors instead of asking people to behave differently while rewarding the old behaviors.

Have clear charters. Competence is a kick. It really is. People naturally want to do well in their work, to achieve their objectives and feel proud of their accomplishments. But they can only seek excellence if they know at what they are expected to excel. When charters are unclear—either poorly defined, too broad, or inconsistent—the innate drive for excellence is suppressed. A healthy design provides a clear definition of each business.

Measure the right things. Every Olympic and business champion uses metrics to assess, track, and improve upon performance. In Motorola, we used the expression, "If you can't measure it, you can't manage it." During its heyday, Motorola was all about metrics…Six Sigma, 10X cycle time reduction, etc. It was the pivotal strategy that led Motorola to being considered one of the finest companies in the world from the mid-1980s to the end of the century.

Establish a performance orientation and monitor performance. Determine ways and means to monitor performance, compare the results with stated objectives, access an evolving database from which to review past actions and base future actions, and determine how to constantly renew the organization's style, systems, and strategy to keep pace with changing conditions.

Measure the degree to which emphasis is placed upon accountability for clearly defined results and high performance. High ratings indicate that people know their accountabilities and the standards for performance. Low ratings may indicate that accountability is defused and unclear or that no one is clearly responsible for producing specific end results.

Consider the extent to which: 1) managers are held personally accountable for the end results they produce or fail to produce; 2) the measures or yardsticks used to judge performance are clear; 3) managers and professionals meet demands for higher performance; and 4) the goals in the organization, department, unit, or project are challenging.

Is it working? How do you know? Would your team say your structure supports or thwarts the achievement of your vision?

In his book *The 8ᵀᴴ Habit*, Stephen R. Covey, author of one of the biggest selling books in history, described a poll of twenty-three thousand employees drawn from a number of companies and industries. He summarized the poll's findings:

- Only 37 percent said they understand what their organization is trying to achieve and why.
- Only one in five was enthusiastic about their team's and organization's goals.
- Only one in five said they had a clear "line of sight" between their tasks and their team's and organization's goals.
- Only 15 percent felt that their organization fully enables them to execute key goals.
- Only 20 percent fully trusted the organization they worked for.

Then Mr. Covey related this to a sports metaphor that links directly to the Olympic performance theme of this book. He said, "If, say, a soccer team had these same scores, only 4 of the 11 players on the field would know which goal is theirs. Only 2 of the 11 would care. Only 2 of the 11 would know what position they play and know exactly what they are supposed to do. And all but 2 players would, in some way, be competing against their own team members rather than the opponent."

Powerful point well made.

Success depends on adaptability, flexibility, and speed. The ability to move decisively in and out of markets, quickly change product features, and add new value overnight are table stakes in today's global marketplace, the price of simply entering the game. Staying ahead means constant, unrelenting change.

Be certain you have measurement systems in place to track the efficiency and effectiveness of the organization. For example, diagnostic processes can help identify, eliminate, or reduce the overlap and duplication that often emerges in decentralized structures. Surveys and other feedback devices should inform the management team of specific problems in the interplay of strategic plans, product/process design, job and organizational designs, and management systems, policies, and procedures. All of these elements impact the commitment and productivity of employees to deliver products, systems, and services. Consequently, in aggregate they measure the extent to which the organization is creating conditions that produce high performance. Leverage these tools. They work.

Create tools and processes to identify and strengthen key organizational, structural, process, and leadership elements. These tools should tell you what is, and is not, working. They should provide cumulative, real-time survey results that are instantly available to key management and participants. This enables identification of issues and immediate problem-solving process while poll findings are still fresh and relevant. As new issues are identified, questions can be developed to capture the group's responses, thereby tailoring the survey results to each group's unique concerns.

These new surveys are not attitude surveys but rather organization practices surveys. Attitude surveys predict morale. Organization practices surveys predict performance. While attitudes are indeed important, the results of organization practices surveys are more informative to the organization about specific problems in the interplay of strategic plans, product/process design, job and organizational designs, and management systems, policies, and procedures. This type of survey measures primarily those organizational factors that have direct relevance to the "bottom line" of performance and over which managers have some degree of control.

Producing enduring systems change is an enormous challenge. But then, if it were easy, every company could do it and it would not represent a competitive advantage. The challenge is to create high-performance systems that propel the organization to higher levels of effectiveness and efficiency. In my corporate experience, these survey processes served as the catalyst for great change with widespread organizational ownership.

Cut the drag in the system. Most change efforts are fragmented. They are isolated techniques or address a component of the whole system. These change efforts are less likely to produce significant or lasting results than an approach that considers elements of the whole system and creates alignment among those elements. Most companies covet an engaged workforce. One of the key antagonists to employee engagement is an organization out of alignment. Likewise for retention. Alignment and organization integration are key.

The whole set of inter-related variables must be carefully managed to effect changes that work in concert, not in conflict.

To ensure total alignment and achieve organizational excellence, the whole set of inter-related variables must be carefully managed to effect changes that work in concert, not in conflict. Sending one message through an explicit vision or strategy statement while sending a conflicting one through the measurement or reward system causes confusion and frustrates positive results. Each element is linked to all the others, with leadership being the pivotal point in the model that energizes the other variables.

Research and practice prove time and again that the key to success in organizational change is designing a total system of improvement in which the key elements are aligned with one another. Dealing with only a piece of the total system while ignoring the impact on the whole is often a fatal flaw among organizations working to affect performance improvement. Picture the elements of an organization on a radar screen. Issues show up as blips in one or more areas, blocking work on important tasks. Air traffic controllers use radar to manage relationships among aircraft—height, speed, distance apart—and to avoid heavy weather. A blip in any one area cannot be managed independently of its relationship to the other areas. Similarly, the whole system of interdependent organizational variables must be addressed.

Key management systems and processes—vision, strategy and objectives, organizational structure, reward systems, and leadership style—must support, not thwart, the business vision. This practice is critical to any organization's success.

Any organization is a complex system of structures, policies, practices, and procedures that interact to influence performance, productivity, and morale. Leading organizations continually analyze and improve upon those drivers of performance. They work aggressively to overthrow existing systems and structures that directly counter high-performance objectives.

Over many years, I have observed companies that were building with one hand and tearing down with the other. Learning professionals would be teaching teamwork, yet the compensation department would recommend "pay for performance" salary or bonus programs that forced individual ranking and encouraged internal competition. The CEO would encourage managers to innovate, but the finance department would evaluate potential new products and projects based upon existing ROI and cost accounting formulas. The human resources organization would establish new initiatives to encourage employees to find better ways of doing their jobs, but the company's information systems were geared to producing historical reports for management. We have all worked in organizations for which this was true and felt the drag on the system.

There are no villains in this picture. Each functional department is trying to do its best under the old rules that said departments function more or less autonomously and that coordination comes from above. However, the rules have changed.

Each element is linked to all the others, and the organization will be only as strong as its weakest link. Thus, the key to success in organization change is designing a total system in which the key elements are aligned with one another.

Of course, high-integrity, ethical behavior from and toward all constituencies (employees, shareholders, communities) must be a non-negotiable expectation for continued employment. Ethical decision-making and responsible governance must be treated as black and white issues. There are no shades of grey.

REDUCE EXCESSIVE BUREAUCRACY

Focus on high-leverage activities and do not let the bureaucracy get in the way. Great competitors concentrate efforts and resources, making sure people spend time where it counts, not stoking the bureaucracy. Yet old-school managers still ask people to waste thousands of potentially productive hours preparing charts for presentations that no one really hears, preparing reports that no one really reads, and attending perfunctory meetings that serve largely as an antidote for insomnia. Management must ensure that the team focuses on work that will produce the greatest payoff.

Misdirected actions waste precious time, deflect focus from the task at hand, and generally take the organization's eye off the ball. Any feedback device will highlight strengths and weaknesses. Before spending time addressing weaknesses, be certain these areas are critical to your competitive advantage.

Tom Peters and Bob Waterman observed long ago in their book *In Search of Excellence* that "left to their own devices, systems evolve to greater levels of complexity, taking on a life of their own. They become more thorough, more detailed, demanding more and more uniformity and controlling more and more of everything. Formal committees with power to grant approvals begin to multiply. Committees drone on. More sign-offs are needed to get anything done.

"Ultimately, these support systems inhibit rather than facilitate performance. They consume the very resources they are designed to protect. People often give up on good ideas because the hoops they must jump through to get something done in the system are so numerous and cumulatively restrictive."

More than three decades later, it is still true that if you obliterate these systems and cut needless bureaucracy, productivity and performance will soar.

Exemplary leaders ensure that the team focuses on work that really matters. They wage war on the bureaucracy, realizing that complex systems and procedures invade the real work of innovating, servicing, and producing with quality. They work aggressively to overthrow existing systems and structures that don't support their business vision. They eliminate (not reduce) excessive paperwork, redundant or inhibiting support functions, and excessive reports, presentations, and meetings.

Focus on business results, not activities...Any change process uncovers activities where performance is outstanding, but irrelevant to the overall business objectives and strategies. Such activities must be abandoned.

CULTURE AND PERFORMANCE REVISITED

Most companies measure the strength of their culture. Great idea. In doing so, consider using surveys that measure key levers that stimulate, produce, and sustain positive change.

These leverage points include clarity of vision, organizational structure, performance management, organization systems, teamwork, and leadership. In sum, these reflect the extent to which a culture and structure have been created to produce high performance.

Remember, the intent of any survey process is not simply to collect data and provide feedback, but rather to generate action plans that result in measurable, positive impact. The survey process should serve as a catalyst to stimulate and sustain change. Resource allocation must be aligned with strategic priorities.

Excessive vertical integration in the organization can create a strong, silo-like mentality—creating significant duplication of effort, overlapping charters, and a self-protective mind-set. The opportunity costs created by the silos are huge in light of the significant white spaces, which are readily recognized by employees at all levels. When charters overlap, people will compete—that is, the structure creates internal territorial battles and precludes effective collaboration. It is not that people naturally want to fight; rather, the organization's structure may create border conflicts by design. To build an atmosphere of cooperation, the design of the organization must ensure clear, distinct charters.

In one company, my team observed deliberate blurring of charters by several members of management in order to foment dissent and distrust at the lower levels. This was a job security strategy for senior management as they could then come in and keep the peace. It was said this dog-eat-dog strategy enabled those at the top to do illicit things without being noticed. We all noticed.

Strategy should lead to structure. How can we shift the strategy without shifting the structure to support it? Why are we not restructuring to reflect strategic changes? The structure selected should be the one that best facilitates the organization's objectives. No other reason should guide the structure!

My thirty years in corporate work suggest leaders who achieve peak performance master the following:

- Create a clear vision for the future direction of the business.
- Ensure that activities and efforts are focused, consistent, and vision-driven.
- Follow a plan rather than jumping from crisis to crisis.
- Eliminate non-value-added activities.
- Clearly define roles and responsibilities.
- Build an organizational structure that fosters clear accountability.
- Eliminate functional and organizational barriers.
- Develop clear and realistic performance goals.
- Delegate responsibility and authority to the lowest appropriate level.
- Establish a positive climate where people are inspired to excel.
- Personally model and exemplify organizational values.

The goal: strength with speed.

The starter's gun fires. Synapses detonate. Hearts race. Boats surge through the water. For minutes, the world is a silent blur, a crucible of speed and will power. Then the sprint is over. To be a winner you can't be fast once in a while—you must be fast every time out. High-performing teams understand that winning is a combination of surpassing form, brilliant technique, and overall excellence. Only by thoroughly mastering a set of disciplines can one hope to compete at the world championship level. The way you organize has a significant impact on speed.

CHAPTER 7

LEADING THE WAY

Leadership strength determines business performance

L eaders lead through their ability and willingness to create a compelling vision, empower their followers, and allocate power into their teams so they have the energy and freedom to innovate. Most importantly, they lead by caring for their followers, which provides emotional commitment and mutual loyalty.

Leaders establish the vision and communicate it in a way that helps people connect their day-to-day work with the organization's strategic objectives. They are resource providers, obstacle removers, facilitators, advisors, and team builders. Leaders generate commitment, not compliance. They envision, empower, and enable—and then get out of the way and let people get results. For much of my career, I have had leaders like this. It is a gift I have treasured.

If leaders strengthened their ability to do those three things—envision, enable, and empower—their employees would require less supervision and

Leaders are obstacle removers, facilitators, advisors, and team builders generating commitment, not compliance.

be more like heat-seeking missiles, aggressively pursuing worthwhile targets established by management. (Employee abilities could be conceptualized as "prepare, promote, and perform.") The hallmark of an excellent leader is the performance of their team!

STAFF FOR HIGH PERFORMANCE

Is your team or organization ready and able to identify, attract, and retain talented people; willing to surround itself with highly capable staff and to encourage individual contributions; staff for and build effective teams committed to organizational goals; and foster collaboration among team members and teams? If so, you are fortunate.

Scouting out top talent is an essential, and difficult, task. You can be a Gold-medal winning Olympian, yet just months earlier, be considered unremarkable.

A member of the U.S. Women's Gymnastics team at the 2012 Summer Olympics, Gabrielle "Gabby" Douglas was the first American gymnast to win Gold in both the individual all-around and team competitions at the

same Olympics. A great feat. But she was not always considered great…
or even Olympic material.

Gabby made her national debut at the 2010 Nastia Liukin Supergirl Cup,
a televised meet held in Worcester, Massachusetts, where she placed
fourth all-around. In October, at age fourteen, Douglas moved from
Virginia Beach, Virginia, to West Des Moines, Iowa, to train under Liang
Chow, the former coach of 2008 Summer Olympics Gold medalist Shawn
Johnson. Chow was initially skeptical because Douglas had been just
one of hundreds of children at the clinic in Virginia Beach where they
first met. Nonetheless, Chow accepted her.

Douglas rose to the challenge and became an Olympic champion. Liang
Chow transformed Douglas into one of the best gymnasts in the world.

Gabby Douglas said she had felt confident all along that she would
win. Yet just five months earlier, Martha Karolyi, the coordinator of the
women's national team, did not think Douglas had what it took to be an
Olympian. Karolyi said Gabby lacked confidence and focus, even just a
few weeks prior to the Olympic Games.

Douglas' improvement during the last several months leading to the
Olympics was so stunning that her victory was not surprising. However,
from the vantage point of a year earlier, her Olympic all-around title
is nothing short of astounding. Karolyi, wife of legendary coach Bela,
has seen many gymnasts in her time. She stated: "I have never seen

a gymnast climb from an average gymnast to the best in the world in five months."

Picking business talent is similarly no easy feat. Most business philosophies are straightforward: increase profitability, control costs and expenses, and grow in strategic areas. The company must invest in its people to compete effectively. Its people are the future as well as the present. Thus, the company must work as hard at assessing, deploying, and developing people as it does developing markets, new plants, and new technologies.

High-performing organizations recruit talented individuals and place them into focused, driven teams. They let their skills, drive, intelligence, and creativity emerge. They create the culture to allow their people to do their best. By doing so, the talents of the Gabby Douglas-like rising stars can shine through.

Select for leadership strength, resilience, and a passion for excellence. These are more important than technical skills. These traits do not always readily appear, like with Bo Jackson (concurrent star of Major League Baseball and National Football League) or the skills emerging in Robert Redford's character, Roy Hobbs, in the movie, *The Natural*. You must assess drive and will to win as well as capacity for exemplary performance. "Fire in the belly" is an indispensable asset. In the course of my career, I have seen many people with ordinary track records perform at extraordinary levels with proper motivation, support, and recognition. Likely, so have you, so pour it on.

The ability to select, develop, motivate, and mobilize a high-performing workforce has a direct impact on business success. The blurring of industry structure—a blurring that results from new technologies and global competitors—has rendered traditional measures of competitive strength—such as production, automation, and marketing skills—potentially obsolete. Hence, a key arena in which to outperform the competition and sustain a unique advantage over them is through the quality of your workforce.

Far too often, there is a shortage of experienced general managers ready to run global, large, complex businesses. Many people in key slots have had little, or no, development. The top team is actively striving to retain their positions. At the next level, there is an ambitious but unproven management team with a paucity of performance evaluation skills and an inability to rate and rank personnel (all are categorized as high performance/high potential, so everyone is a superstar, and yet bench-strength is lacking). This can cascade downward.

This leadership shortage may be due to a lack of priority setting, poor or non-existent leadership programs or processes, inadequate support systems, a poor skill/experience mix, or inappropriate measurement and reward mechanisms. Work to shore up these enablers.

Driving change requires leaders who can energize and inspire people. Such leaders must personify the organization's purpose—through a style and skill-set that reflects the quality of the leader's values, thinking, and character—to inspire a commitment to the leader's strategy and goals and to secure the allegiances required to make any bold purpose succeed. Put the best qualified person in each position.

Always seek to be known as an organization that attracts the best minds in the industry and you will attract more great minds. Likewise, always seek to be known as a great leader who inspires exemplary performance. By working together and continuing to pinpoint areas where you need to change and work smarter and better, you can move confidently into the new business world. Your organization will continue to face rapid changes and challenges. The contributions of key leaders driving ahead to new levels of excellence will provide you with the leading edge.

Change rewrites job descriptions. Therefore, start from scratch in assessing your people. Approach this endeavor as if all employees were new hires. Even incumbents will face new demands, and you need to evaluate their adaptability. Ask yourself if some of them should be repositioned. Is it possible some good people are poorly suited for their evolving positions?

Size up your team with an objective, discerning eye. Look for strengths, improvement opportunities, goals, preferences, experience, and areas of expertise. The keener your insights into each individual, the better you can manage and lead them effectively.

Selection is one of the most important controls a manager has. Yet in this vital area, many enterprises remain weak for one or more of many reasons:

- Bright, talented individuals are moved too quickly and not left in their jobs long enough to substantially develop skills.
- Placements are based on style, loyalty, social relationships, or political connections rather than primarily on performance, competence, and job fit.
- The selection process is ignored or passes up highly qualified individuals to fill positions.
- Little knowledge exists across divisions and functions about available, qualified candidates.
- Little is known about the aspirations of high potentials. Decisions are often based upon assumptions about their aspirations rather than their stated desires.
- When evaluating managers, we tend to categorize them based upon past images rather than current performance.

Do a self-assessment to determine if you have any improvement opportunities with respect to the above list. Emphasize cleaner evaluations of performance and potential. While discussions about performance characteristics of incumbents and their potential are becoming more frank and realistic, people tend to backslide when pressed to fill a job. Be careful. Also, certain managers have a tendency to act as sponsors or mentors for all people in their organizations. This should be modulated.

Seek and select people with special leadership qualities: the ability to see and articulate a clear, compelling vision and mission, the will to maintain the course, the courage to take a long-range perspective, the willingness to empower others to remove impediments, the capability to display optimism, confidence, and courage. These leaders have the ability to bring in the best people…and bring out the best in people.

LEADERS GROWING LEADERS

The patterns of leadership become very clear over time. True leaders are quickly separated from those who are not leaders by a core set of beliefs and actions. They identify, attract, and retain the most talented, diverse group of high performers. They understand the core competencies and skills required to meet challenging business goals, and they surround themselves with highly capable staff.

In the late 1990s and beyond, the entire business community was talking about the McKinsey study on the "War for Talent." CEOs made pronouncements of strategic intent to win on this battlefield. Vision statements were revised to emphasize acquiring and developing human capital. Companies made big promises. They made a commitment to attract and retain world-class people, promising to create an environment in which people wanted to, and could, perform at the highest levels of their potential.

Further, they would bolster recruiting strategies, create leading-edge development programs, and focus relentlessly on retaining highly talented, motivated, and productive teams. They couldn't do enough for their people.

Over time, however, as a challenging business climate lingered, these promises were not kept in many organizations. Though their Annual Reports proclaimed people to be their "most important assets," people were often treated as a liability, not an asset. Company after company reacted to short-term pressures by pushing the "pause" button on development of human capital. One hardly heard about the War for Talent any longer.

There are significant lessons to be learned from recent economic down-turns. As we look back, we learn that the companies that weathered the storms and came out on top practiced what they preached. They acted on their belief that during times of both prosperity and uncertainty, success hinges on the quality of a company's leadership…at all levels of the organization.

Those that invested in their human capital typically outperformed the field. The other companies allowed themselves to be diverted. They focused on trying **not to lose**, which is wholly different that **trying to win**. Those firms have more ground to cover now.

In good times and bad, there has always been, and will always be, a War for Talent. Acquiring, building, supporting, and leveraging a high-performance workforce has never been more critical for profitable growth or customer satisfaction.

You cannot have a great company unless you have great leaders in the company. And the best leaders have a deep commitment to building leadership talent throughout the organization. In fact, they regard this as an obligation and a privilege.

These leaders encourage development by rewarding excellence, serving as role models, and encouraging growth. They push decision-making to the lowest appropriate level and develop subordinates' confidence in their ability to lead, manage, and impact business results. They allocate sufficient authority and resources to subordinates to enable them to make significant decisions and act independently within their area of responsibility. These are the primary drivers of development.

Growth occurs primarily as a function of challenging experiences on the job, and not in the classroom. Ultimately, great leaders achieve business objectives by finding, nurturing, and developing leaders who champion change, innovation, and continuous improvement; they are expert at leveraging leadership capability across business groups, fostering

---

Leaders encourage development by rewarding excellence, serving as role models, and encouraging growth. They push decision-making to the lowest appropriate level.

cross-organizational learning, and building unity, alignment, and capacity for execution amongst leadership teams at all levels of the organization. They view these activities as a source of sustainable competitive advantage.

Companies that continue to invest in their talent even during tough times are better positioned to take advantage of recovering markets. These companies act upon their belief that people are an organization's critical strategic advantage, and while remaining focused on the present, they invest their time and money planning for the future—selecting, developing, and retaining the next generation of business leaders. They use challenging times as a chance to better position their leadership and organization for the future.

Look around and you will find solid examples of "best-practice" companies. These are the companies with a decades-long commitment to high-performance succession, executive, and leadership development practices. They ensure they have the right people with the right skills and motivations in the right jobs at the right time. They set the course and stay the course. Their talent review, management, and succession processes are institutionalized throughout the business. They are conducted without fail every quarter, each time expecting a higher level of excellence.

Accordingly, these companies actually strengthen their position in attracting and retaining the best talent even during these tough times. This practice further sets these companies apart from their competitors and makes them a magnet for talent. They serve as great role models.

A high-performing, productive work force facilitates attainment of short-term profit goals as well as long-term strategic objectives. Believe in the strength, capacity, and potential for growth and contribution of your people. Developing leaders is either viewed as a cost or as an investment. Small decisions broadcast whether you believe in human capital development or simply spout empty promises. The impact of these decisions is long-lasting.

In an era of constant change, the only competitive advantage you have is your ability to learn *faster* than your competitors. Managers and professionals must develop the mindsets, skills, and abilities to cope with the flux. Developing competencies is key to gaining competitive advantage; ensuring the identification and satisfaction of development needs in the context of current and future jobs; providing a challenging climate to encourage people development by rewarding excellence, serving as a role model, and encouraging personal and professional growth; and making it possible to devote your time and resources to developmental activities in the face of competing pressures.

Ultimately, you own your own development—the ball is in your court! When participants in my executive development programs completed the process, I presented them with a canister of tennis balls. Why, after giving seemingly weightier awards earlier, did we go lightweight with tennis balls for leadership? The answer lies in the message etched on each ball: "The ball is in my court."

Leaders must make this pledge: "I will remove impediments to success and display optimism, confidence, and courage. I will stick my neck out, try new approaches to management and make them work. I will exercise my courage. I will stake my reputation, even my job, to bring about change—and throw myself into it with a verve and commitment. I will be aware of obstacles, complexities, uncertainties, and challenges but choose to instead to see opportunities. When I find a problem, I will seek to fix the problem. I won't wait to be empowered—I will empower myself. When I see a problem that requires a solution, a challenge that needs to be seized, or an opportunity that should be exploited, I won't look up, look down, or look for the perfect moment, I will just do it! The ball is in my court!"

Organizations and leaders that win in coming years will understand the changes affecting them and seize them, master them, and use them to their advantage to achieve ever-higher performance. The talent, drive, energy, and commitment of your people will give you an edge over your competition: your people are your leading edge. Your leadership of them can stimulate incredible levels of performance.

Create a platform for exceptional execution and profitable growth: talent management, organizational design, culture building, executive continuity, and performance management. Use these disciplines as platforms for continuous renewal.

Most companies do not seize opportunities prompted by change because they do not see the opportunities prompted by change. They're too busy making the most of yesterday's opportunities to make the most of today's or create tomorrow's. By pinpointing areas where you need to change and working smarter and better, you can move confidently into the new business world. If not now…when? If not you…who?

Now, you may ask, how can we best develop our leaders?

The best companies commit to initiatives designed to develop high-performance leaders. These programs, processes, and policies enable sustained performance excellence by building a leadership team across boundaries of geography and business, and they function with a clear, common vision and strategy for its achievement.

Noteworthy leadership programs focus on different management skill-levels and use a combination of company presenters, external world-class subject matter experts, electronic learning technologies, and post-program project work to reinforce key strategic initiatives. Participants compare

---

Most companies do not *seize* opportunities prompted by change because they do not see the opportunities prompted by change.

---

the state-of-the-practice in their company with the *state-of-the-art* in the world. Relevant gaps are noted, assessed, and eliminated. They are engaged as both learners and teachers supported in their responsibility to promote the company culture and direction.

Carefully crafted leadership programs enable a company to focus on common challenges, create a unified perspective, and provide management tools to enhance its competitive advantage. When leaders train and work together, they create a foundation for effective change management. This approach provides key people with the same learning experience, a common vocabulary, shared skill-building, and mutual reinforcement. It creates stronger, more cohesive teams, serving as a network-building event in which managers work together in a unique environment that fosters better long-term relationships.

I have seen great impact from programs designed as integrated and cumulative learning processes. Each program is built upon the principles of a prior program and leads to the next programs. By meeting regularly, participants are able to digest the principles articulated in the sessions and have ample opportunity to apply what is being taught. They also become more of a team. The leadership development process is a long-term process and a personally demanding one. Management requests that participants make sessions a number-one priority and work commitments around the program schedule.

There are a host of other strategies:

Delegation and empowerment. Push decision-making to the lowest appropriate level to develop people's confidence in their ability to lead and impact outcomes. Instill a sense of ownership of the business, allocating sufficient authority and resources to enable people to make decisions and act independently within their area of responsibility.

Learning design and process. Design an integrated and cumulative learning process. Each module is built upon the principles of a prior module and leads to the next module. This long-term process (not program) is demanding for each participant. Make attendance at sessions a top priority; work other commitments around the schedule.

Real action learning. Program participants work in focused teams that interface directly with executive management to address real-time business issues. The issues should be significant, not make-work. The executive teams identify, define, and frame issues for program participants to address. Executive champions serve as sponsors, mentors, and bureaucracy-busters. At Motorola, we used this strategy to focus on and improve global growth, cost reduction, customer satisfaction, and cycle time reduction.

Follow-up coaching and feedback with each participant will enhance skill development and ensure that new practices are applied at work. Participants should be assisted on a one-on-one basis in constructively assessing and improving upon their professional style and effectiveness.

Great leaders reward excellence, serve as role models, and encourage personal and professional growth. They believe in the strength, capacity, and potential for growth and contribution of their people.

We must learn to change, to progress, to set stretch goals, to make key decisions faster. We need better ways of measuring and rewarding our people for doing what's right, for making constructive changes, and for taking risks. We can, and will, strive for ever-higher levels of performance excellence.

CHAPTER 8

DEVELOPING THE NEXT GENERATION

Shaping the future

Great leaders focus on the same basic issues: Do we have a clear, compelling vision? Do we have a winning strategy for competitive advantage? Do we have the best team in place? Do we have in place the best person for every position? Are we maximizing the impact and output of our people? Are they working together as a team? Are their activities riveted to the vision? That is what great leaders focus on. They transform their people and culture to take the company to the next level and beyond. Are you doing great work in this area? Do you know what is needed to elevate your game?

Often, these leaders partner with internal or external experts who are skilled and experienced in the disciplines of organization design and integration as well as executive and leadership development and succession planning to create and sustain a competitive advantage. My teams and I have spent thousands of hours over the years working on just those issues.

In the fall of 2013, the Institute of Executive Development and the Rock Center for Corporate Governance at Stanford University conducted in-depth interviews with executives and directors at twenty companies regarding their succession and executive development practices. The following are some key findings of this study headed by Scott Saslow of the Rock Center:

- **In striking contrast to how we did these processes at Motorola, companies often do not know who is next in line to fill senior executive positions.** Organizations often do not make the connection between the skills and experiences required to run the company and the individual candidates—both internal and external—who are best suited to eventually assume senior executive positions. When a list of possible successors is compiled, it is often narrow in scope and therefore not relied on when a succession event actually occurs. At Motorola, we measured actual succession moves made according to the plan. If we picked someone who was *not* a planned successor, it was required that the hiring manager explain the rationale for the change, for example, to inject new capabilities.

- **Again, in stark contrast to how we orchestrated these processes at Motorola, companies studied do not have an actionable process in place to select senior executives.** Companies recognize the importance of a thorough and rigorous succession process for both the CEO and senior executive positions; however, most fail to create one. More about how it was done—always—at Motorola follows. The problem tends to be cultural: the majority of companies do not have honest and open discussions about executive performance, nor do they allocate sufficient time to the process of identifying and grooming successors.

- **In dissonance with our Motorola practices, the Stanford researchers found companies plan for succession to "reduce risk" rather than to "find the best successors."** Succession is essentially a preparation exercise for the future. However, respondents are more likely to view this activity in terms of its potential to reduce future *downside* risk rather than producing shareholder value from the identification of strong and appropriate leadership. This is due in part to the scrutiny of regulators, rating agencies, and other market participants that emphasize the risk management and loss-minimization aspects—rather than the value-creating elements—of succession. During my eleven years at Motorola, we planned for succession just as precisely as we planned any other strategy and with the rigor of the budgeting process.

- **In their survey population, succession plans are not connected with coaching and internal talent development programs.** Succession planning and internal talent development are treated as distinct activities rather than one continuous program to gradually develop leadership skills in the organization. Because of this, the board of directors does not have sufficient insight into the skills and capabilities of the senior management team and is not prepared to determine which executives are most qualified to replace an outgoing CEO or C-suite member when a vacancy is approaching. More on our Motorola disciplines, then regarded as "world-class," follows.

It is imperative that forward-thinking companies address these deficiencies. Here are smart and actionable strategies suggested by the executives at the Rock Center:

- **Cast a wide net.** Because an organization and its strategy are constantly evolving, the skills needed to run the organization in the future are not necessarily the same as they are presently. Executive talent should be evaluated in terms of its ability to meet future—not just past or current—needs. Accordingly, the board and senior management should look broadly through the ranks of the organization to ensure they are fostering a diverse set of talents and skills to take the organization forward. Internal executives should be benchmarked against the external market for talent.

- **Be comprehensive and continuous.** Succession should be treated as an ongoing activity in which management and the board prepare for transitions at any time and at multiple levels throughout the organization. This includes not only the CEO position, but also his or her direct reports, their direct reports, and other critical positions. Contingencies for these positions should be continuously maintained. Succession is more time-consuming, riskier, and more expensive when carried out *following* a departure than in *advance* of one.

Through the years, my teams have found it is critical to build an enterprise-wide perspective in all potential leaders. World-class leaders ensure they use cross-functional exposure, rotation, and task-force involvement to broaden their "stars." They promote information sharing, reduce functional myopia, and promote sharing of management talent across boundaries. Decentralization creates challenges in moving people across business borders. There is a tendency to hoard high potentials and build moats to thwart poaching. You can curb this tendency by several means: The CEO/COO can ensure a balanced focus on leadership development and business needs and move people across boundaries.

Rotations can be funded from a corporate pool for the duration of rotational assignments. Systems can be installed that encourage senior managers to contribute to the success of the entire company, not just their function.

Cross-functional experience helps build flexible mindsets, facilitates the transfer of knowledge and skills, enhances career development, increases retention rate, improves employee satisfaction, boosts employability, and increases the connectivity of employees.

When making job decisions, consider all possible candidates—not simply the person in immediate reporting line-of-sight. Create lists of possible candidates for each opening, including people from outside the business unit and company.

THE NEXUS OF STRATEGY, ORGANIZATION, AND LEADERSHIP

Over the years, my teams organized under the umbrellas of *Quality of Organization* and *Quality of Leadership. Quality of Organization* work was designed to ensure the organization developed the clarity of vision, organizational structure, performance management processes, systems, leadership, and culture to stimulate and sustain high performance. This served to strengthen the extent to which our clients developed the processes, systems, teamwork, and leadership to achieve their business vision.

Quality of Leadership initiatives created a process of identifying, developing, and tracking key executives, high potentials, and key contributors. Our team developed a suite of proprietary tools and processes to achieve superior performance in these areas. These processes received high praise for enabling our clients to achieve their intended objectives.

Throughout my career, I have had senior corporate responsibility for succession-planning, along with several other functions. We had a long list of objectives for succession-planning:

- Align leadership model with the organization's strategy for competitive advantage.
- Contemplate the organization's future scenarios (e.g., markets, customers, products, market position, technology, financial resources, competitive position).
- Determine key business issues with organizational implications and determine planned structural change.
- Use a clear, consistent leadership model as the common framework for discussing leadership behaviors across all businesses and regions.
- Provide ample opportunity for divisions and staff functions to select their specific additional competencies.
- Communicate the leadership expectations and explain the linkage to key result areas, promotions, and compensation.
- Highlight the positions with solid back-up support.

- Designate positions where there is a replacement urgency or need.
- Review key executives and high potentials and accelerate their development.
- Evaluate leadership depth and succession capability.

We encouraged executive management to be fully invested in developing the next generation of leaders. We devised systems to hold managers accountable for demonstrating behaviors that would build the organization's leadership talent pool.

The punch list of imperative actions follows:

- Engage senior management in a disciplined, rigorous, and consistent process of reviewing talent in the context of current and projected business opportunities and challenges.
- Strengthen the focus on organization structure and planned change.
- Review key executives and high-potentials and accelerate their development and/or reevaluate their placement. For each individual, evaluate strengths, improvement needs, and development plans.
- Ensure top talent is matched to critical jobs. Surface "must move/should move" candidates.
- Discuss successors to key positions to surface bench

strength, succession gaps and blockages, key vacancies, and development opportunities.

- Improve the identification and visibility of high-potential candidates through earlier, increased exposure to multiple key business executives.
- Create development plans that are specific, realistic, and have an expected completion date and an assigned responsibility.

Payoffs include:

- A top team with breadth of experience and enterprise-wide perspective.
- Enhanced skills/capabilities to execute against the evolving strategy.
- A disciplined, open and inclusive talent review process.
- Leaders fully invested in developing next generation leadership talent.
- Enhanced top team skills in motivating a high-performance workforce.
- Increased job satisfaction due to better job/skill match.
- Collaboration and coordination across the enterprise.
- Development of an overall scorecard on your organization's bench strength.
- Assured continuity of leadership.

Our path-to-goal accomplishment, from Corporate to the Divisions follows,

"Emphasis will be placed on the Organization and Management Development Review (OMDR) process to identify, develop, and track key executives and high-potentials and to ensure that your organization has the structure and processes to stimulate and sustain superior performance. The OMDR process is comprised of regularly scheduled interviews, discussions, and rigorous assessment and analysis. Emphasis is placed upon candid and realistic evaluations of performance and potential of the current and next generations of leadership. The process will broaden the base of qualified candidates considered and enhance the quality of assessment on each candidate by providing multiple perspectives. Further, it promotes real-time scenario planning.

"The OMDR is conducted in a sequenced process, 'rolling up' to provide the next level of management with the information they need for their respective submittals. Each successively higher level of management can choose to procure information through a paper-based process, by meeting one-on-one with key subordinates, or by meeting in a facilitated Roundtable with broader input on each candidate and an opportunity to consider others not in one's usual line-of-sight."

METRICS FOR DRIVING ACCOUNTABILITY

We designed, installed, and implemented systems that would increasingly hold line managers accountable for building the organization and its leadership talent. These systems would be tailored to the organization. Our clients, the key executives, forged ahead with a tight link between people leadership and organization integration/ effectiveness, promotion, and compensation. Leadership was an unavoidable "gate" for promotion. You could not get promoted based upon the numbers only. The quality of the culture you created and perpetuated was just as important.

The most enlightened key executives believe that to ensure effective executive development, succession systems must match executives to needed development experiences, balance the short-term risks of stretch assignments with their long-term benefits, and selectively enable the enterprise-wide mobility of talent.

There is clear evidence of this. "High Impact Succession Management" by the Corporate Leadership Council of the Corporate Executive Board notes that succession management efforts are not discrete events, but rather part of an integrated system for managing talent in an organization. Leading HR organizations base development and succession decisions on the evolving needs of the company, overcoming both structural rigidity and misalignment between strategic priorities and talent capabilities.

Surveys of CEOs consistently point out that the top factors most important to their success in five years are: developing and retaining potential leaders; top management succession; and talent identification and growth. Accordingly, key executives are now evaluated and compensated in part based upon the extent to which their directs reach excellent rankings in "job fit," meeting or exceeding targeted business objectives, and in generating effective organizational, culture, and leadership survey results.

Further, they are evaluated and compensated against objectives around "successor quality and readiness" and "high potential identification." This evaluation takes into account such factors as the percentages of key incumbents and successors whose planned development activities occur; vacancies filled via the plan; key positions designated with at least one consensually validated "ready now" backup; key positions designated with at least one consensually validated longer-term backup.

RESULTS: COMPETITIVE ADVANTAGE

Over time, these leadership initiatives can be a great differentiator. Clearly, a company's structure, executive readiness, processes for creating and sustaining a high-performance culture, and ability to staff with the best people are required competencies for future success. These activities pay off.

A plethora of studies over the years confirms this in spades. A study by the Hay Group, the University of Michigan, and the Strategic Planning Institute related HR practices to ROI. Business units were compared against a par ROI derived from the earnings recorded for businesses in similar strategic positions. Firms with established succession planning programs for the top three levels of management enjoyed a 15 percent advantage above par ROI over firms lacking a formal program (and business units that lacked a formal succession planning system achieved an ROI 7 percent or worse than par ROI).

The Corporate Leadership Council (CLC) studied 276 organizations worldwide to understand their practices, processes, and expected outcomes in leadership development and succession management. They concluded that "Top Tier Leadership Organizations" delivered 10 percent greater total shareholder return. Top tier was a measurement of executive performance against business goals as well as select qualitative metrics. "Bottom tier" leadership organizations delivered 6 percent lower returns.

Such impact is also cited by consulting firms. Human capital initiatives are increasingly measured by their impact on business and financial outcomes. There is a clear trend toward linking the business impact (margins, growth, cycle time reduction, RONA, customer retention) with successful implementation of human capital initiatives in addition to the usual outcomes (satisfaction, engagement, retention).

Leading companies are putting these practices to good use. Coca-Cola is a highly decentralized company that uses Talent Roundtables as a tool to enhance visibility across business units. Starbucks, Dell, and TRW offer high quality global leadership development programs. Companies such as GE, Pepsi, Motorola, and HP have a decades-long commitment to succession planning and leadership development.

In my corporate experience, open-forum roundtables have been proven to increase the quality and quantity of input, resulting in up to 60 percent revisions to plans made without such input. Ultimately, the objective is to institutionalize a simple, consistent process across the company that has the same rigor as the budget process. Key managers will get briefings and dashboards updating them on the status of these key initiatives.

Consider holding quarterly (at least) roundtable meetings to discuss successors to key positions; to surface key vacancies and developmental opportunities; to identify and plan development actions for high potentials; and to surface must-move/should-move candidates to address job fit and career aspirations. Link succession plans to the business strategy to ensure synergy and leverage.

An effective development strategy integrates career development, on-the-job experience, and formal training and education. A good career development system helps people to identify career paths. The system encourages managers and employees to target specific jobs, pinpoint relevant strengths and limitations, and construct an action plan that links identified needs to specific training or development activities.

Encourage career development through on-the-job experiences by providing systematic exposure to various functional areas through job rotation and periodic evaluation and review of performance. Encourage job enrichment by providing opportunities for professional growth by delegating more responsibility and authority and enlarging jobs (making the job structurally larger by adding duties).

While professional skills are primarily learned on the job, formal classroom training can stimulate professional activity and bring new perspectives, knowledge, and confidence to the job. In the company of colleagues, removed from the normal working environment with its attendant pressures, participants can pursue new concepts energetically and reflect upon their roles. Such self-renewal should not be restricted to a specific point in time, but occur at regular intervals and at appropriate career points to meet changing job requirements and sustain personal growth, implant learning-to-learn skills, and promote professional development.

Successful development programs enjoy long-term management commitment and support, the personal involvement of supervisors, integration with goals, realistic learning objectives based upon assessment of needs, active participation of trainees, guided self-evaluation of progress and accomplishment, opportunities for on-the-job practice, feedback on performance, and learning activities of sufficient depth, variety, and coverage to be challenging.

KEEP THE FIRES BURNING

How can you keep people engaged, excited, and motivated?

- **Provide meaningful work.** Meaningful work stimulates the intellect.

- **Encourage involvement in decisions and activities.** Give managers autonomy to carry out their responsibilities.

Allow them to make decisions using their experience and knowledge. Be unobtrusive with the controls you place on their activities. Find methods to use their experience and knowledge in ways that go beyond their jobs. Place them on task forces or committees. Their experience and wisdom may be useful, and participation will build their commitment.

- **Foster teaching and coaching.** Because longer-service executives identify with the company and are concerned about the next generation, they can serve as teachers, mentors, and coaches. Beyond developing younger people, these roles meet the psychological needs of plateaued managers. By allowing them to make this contribution, they will understand they are necessary to the future of the company.

- **Stretch the job.** Add new challenges or responsibilities or reassign tasks for everyone's benefit. You can also stretch people by giving them more temporary assignments, such as service on task forces and problem-solving committees.

- **Create new growth opportunities in many ways, including:** cross-functional bridges that expand job parameters; lateral moves that can provide new challenges and new environment; work on project teams and temporary groups; and special assignments such as task force problem-solving teams that take little time yet add responsibility, challenge, and recognition.

Most people need continuous growth opportunities to stay motivated. People who have such opportunities respond with high aspirations, self-confidence, a strong task focus, and constructive attitudes. Provide them with a meaningful job that allows them a feeling of achievement, responsibility, growth, advancement, and recognition.

In the event of lackluster performance or the presence of a rising star eclipsing an employee's development, what alternatives are there to retirement or termination? Not all employees can rise steadily in the ranks (the up-or-out attitude). We must allow people to reach plateaus in jobs where they can perform ably without being promoted into positions where they can't perform well. They should be allowed to move laterally to other positions that suit their abilities. A good engineer may be a poor manager. An assertive and bright person who is promoted too rapidly into management may welcome a less demanding job that offers career stability.

Most people rust out before they wear out. The aim of revitalizing people is to renew their skills and recharge their motivational drive. If the source of ineffectiveness lies primarily in stagnation, the challenge of a new position (lateral transfer) may be needed to boost performance.

Outside programs offer stimulation through exposure to other managers with a wide range of experience and backgrounds who communicate new perspectives and fresh approaches.

CHAPTER 9

RECOGNIZE SUPERIOR PERFORMANCE

Measure and reward superior performance

During the original Olympic Games in ancient Greece, champions were not awarded gold, silver, and bronze medals as they are today. Instead, ancient Olympic victors were awarded an olive branch twisted into a circle to form a crown. The wild olive, called **kotinos**, had deep religious significance for the ancient Greeks. At the ancient Olympics, only the champion was recognized—there were no prizes for runners up.

Most of us can recall seeing Olympic medal ceremonies. The sight of a triumphant Olympic athlete receiving the Gold medal as his or her country's national anthem plays is one of the most moving images of each Olympiad. World-class performance should be recognized. Every competitor's life-long dream is to win a medal, preferably Gold.

In business, the reward system also signals to every member of the organization what management truly wants, values, and recognizes.

It was this dream that inspired thousands of hours of drills and years of workouts, calorie-counting, and other sacrifices to earn this recognition.

In business, the reward system also signals to every member of the organization what management truly wants, values, and recognizes. Be sure to use the most potent types of recognition you have to reward innovative leaders. A mandate for change will produce heroes—people who stick their necks out, trying new approaches to management and making them work. They place themselves at the forefront of change, in the eye of the storm—and they may actually create the storm. Others watch to see if they are rewarded or punished for their risk-taking. Are these heroes promoted and rewarded—or punished?

Be certain that highly principled behavior is rewarded. This seems axiomatic. Of course we reward integrity, honesty, and transparency. However, this is not always the case. For example, many of the companies that caused the economy to crater with shoddy loans and exotic investment products, both of which vaporized in value, rewarded going along with the flow, even if the flow was in the general direction of fraud, deceit, and duplicity. Further, people reported being punished for refusing to engage in fraud, deceit, or corruption. I was close to the action on this. It was true.

Know that what gets rewarded gets repeated; what gets punished gets extinguished. You will get more of what gets rewarded. You will get less of what gets punished. Please choose wisely and honorably. Be certain to reward "the right stuff."

Consider the extent to which:

1. People believe there are strong incentives to achieve excellent results.
2. Compensation, recognition, and promotion are directly related to performance, and the rewards are both adequately and fairly administered.
3. Poor performance will be penalized, but management is not punitive or abusive.
4. Genuine personal satisfaction can be realized both through personal achievement and outstanding organizational performance.

High scores in this dimension mean employees believe that the organization's reward system is competitive compared with other employers; that the system is internally equitable; and that rewards are commensurate with performance—or perhaps all three.

In some firms, decisions on promotion, rotation, and pay are more a function of seniority or conformity than performance. This is counterproductive and sends all the wrong signals.

Achieving high productivity, quality, and innovation requires professionals who are capable and motivated and who want the job and can do the job. If promotions, rotations, and raises are based on seniority rather than on performance, the signal is to slow down and stick around.

Use rewards to fuel high performance. People behave in ways that earn them meaningful rewards. To be effective, positive reinforcement must satisfy three conditions:

Consistency. Important rewards must be tightly linked to effective performance. Performance is the consistent ability to produce results over time and in a variety of assignments. High-performing organizations (HPOs) use people decisions (placement, pay, promotions, demotions, and firings) to signal what management really wants, values, and rewards. Sadly, decisions on promotion, rotation, and pay are often more a function of seniority, conformity, or friendship than performance. HPOs reward all who perform at a high level, rather than allocate rewards along a normal distribution curve.

Potency. Successful companies determine what motivates each person (money, pat-on-the-back, promotion, appreciation). They are zealous about catching people doing the right things and doing things right and celebrate even small successes with great fanfare. The best way to motivate people to work effectively is to provide them with a meaningful job that allows freedom of achievement, responsibility, growth, advancement, and recognition. However, in days of retrenchment, budget constraints, and radical downsizing, companies must use the vast arsenal of motivational tools in creative ways to stimulate high performance. People will often go to great lengths to earn token symbols of achievement of appreciation. Changes in job title or assignment, employee-of-the-month awards, certificates, and a congratulatory letter for achievement all have a powerful effect on performance.

Immediacy. The closer the reinforcement is to the behavior, the greater the odds the behavior will increase. Annual merit increases don't provide immediate reinforcement for performance. Find ways to immediately reinforce high performance. Rewards in real-time increase peak performance!

Reward talented contributors who model vision-driven, values-based behavior (as opposed to those who are turf-protecting, politically motivated, and unresponsive to task assignments). People quickly form perceptions about the rewards available and the extent to which they are related to performance. High scores in this dimension mean employees believe that the reward system is competitive and fair and that rewards are commensurate with performance. I have seen people flourish just by noting this linkage. How would you grade your own efforts in this area?

The highly respected Society for Human Resources (SHRM)/Globoforce Spring 2013 Report concluded that there has been a noted rise in recognition programs, and companies are seeing proven business benefits from recognizing great work and performance. There is overwhelming support for investing more in "praise and prize." You can be a role model in this area. Investing here will yield huge returns.

KNOW WHEN TO HOLD 'EM; KNOW WHEN TO FOLD 'EM

What if you are not getting good performance? Before you proceed to a counseling session with the employee, you must decide what you are willing and able to do to correct the problem.

A reality of life is that growth stops; people hit a plateau, lose motivation, energy, and/or skill; promotional opportunities dry up; jobs cease to be challenging; jobs become obsolete; and both the individual and the organization are eventually faced with the prospect of disengagement in reality or "retiring on the job."

Individuals identified as marginal performers need to be given immediate special management attention. Marginal performance must be faced squarely by management and resolved by increased goal clarity and support, performance-enhancing coaching and counseling, reassignment, training and education, or replacement. The process begins with the identification of marginal performers and pinpointing the reasons for the performance problem. Then a definitive improvement plan should be established, agreed upon, and monitored closely. If after a reasonable period of time there is no evidence of noticeable improvement in performance, arrange to remove or outplace the person.

Managers must sincerely examine the situation to see if organizational support, so necessary for success, is lacking. Individual performance is a function of goal clarity, supportive organization structure, adequate resources, required skills, performance-enhancing feedback, motivation, relationship with supervisor, and a host of other factors. The problem may be more of inadequate management direction or resources than employee willingness or ability. In this case, the situation can be remedied.

Too often, plateaued managers who have quit emotionally are seen as likely candidates to eliminate. What is often overlooked is that these long-service employees may form the cores of organizations that produce the day-to-day results. Instead of considering how to eliminate such people, perhaps a more relevant question is: how can we keep them excited and motivated in the second halves of their careers?

Continuing real opportunity is the motivator most people need to keep them working with a high degree of effort and enthusiasm. People who have real opportunity respond with high aspirations, self-confidence, a strong task focus, and constructive attitudes.

While competent managers who become "unnecessary" because of organizational changes can frequently be reassigned within the company, this is clearly not the case for unsuccessful or incompetent individuals. When dealing with an unsatisfactory individual, management must take a good hard look at the person and, when necessary, properly prepare for his/her termination.

Unfortunately, incompetent and unsatisfactory managers and executives are frequently kept on far longer than they should be, seriously undermining the success and the viability of the company. Although management has the basic tools and systems at its disposal to properly evaluate the abilities and competencies of personnel, many do not do a good job of appraising employees.

Rooting out poor performers will foster a climate of continual improvement. The human tendency to avoid confrontation allows companies to fall into the trap of complacency and subpar performance. Upgrading the organization, by contrast, requires managers to make tough decisions: to fire some people, demote or bypass others, and tell poor performers where they stand. No one enjoys delivering bad news. It's not fun. However, good managers understand how critical it is to the company's long-term success.

Those who consistently render poor or mediocre performance should be removed from their jobs for their own good. People who work in jobs that exceed their capabilities and capacities are frustrated, harassed,

You can never strengthen the weak by weakening the strong.

anxiety-ridden, and ineffective. We do not do people a service by placing them in jobs to which they are not equal. We do them a disservice. Not to face up to a person's failure in a job is cowardice, not compassion.

You also owe it to the person's subordinates, who have a right to be managed with competence, dedication, and achievement. Subordinates have a right to a manager who performs, for otherwise they themselves cannot perform. You also owe it to all the people in the organization not to put up with a manager who fails to perform.

In my early career, I was confronted with just this situation. My team was growing quickly so I promoted my most senior subject matter expert to a management position. Six months later, it was clear his people-skills left much to be desired. I coached him, trained him, and gave him feedback. I gave him time to improve, perhaps too much. Nothing worked. Moreover, his former status was diminished as seen by prior admirers. I regretted having to counsel him out of his position but did so after some delay. However, as his functional skills were strong, I returned him to a position that played to his strengths. Months later, he told me he was thrilled to return to a staff position.

You can never strengthen the weak by weakening the strong. The goal is to recruit, develop, train, and motivate people to become leaders in their professions and position. Yet management frustration intensifies with feast-and-famine hiring, abrupt hiring freezes, a perceived no-lay-off policy for long-service employees, and frozen replacement requisitions.

AN OUNCE OF PREVENTION IS WORTH A POUND OF CURE

When you find that an individual's work is unsatisfactory, make every attempt for a reasonable time to upgrade the person's performance with developmental counseling, coaching, and training.

Identify and discuss critical success factors and incidents that illustrate unsatisfactory performance. Examine the situation to see if support is lacking.

Set clear performance standards. Promotion-from-within policies and clear standards for promotion encourage individuals who do not meet those standards to confront their low promotion potential and take corrective action or withdraw to a more suitable organization. Career counselors and outside placement counselors can help people establish realistic career expectations and facilitate the departure of surplus and less effective employees.

Clarify objectives: review the current plans in effect, revising any that are clearly unattainable. Then publish the new plan and communicate to all that these are now the objectives they are expected to achieve. Each team member must be clear on their responsibilities and have a clear understanding of the standards of performance on each responsibility. Create a set of performance objectives for the year to which you both agree and insist that they execute.

Tighten discipline: high-performance teams are disciplined. The team members are strict with themselves, and they execute with precision. My respect for the 1990s Chicago Bulls went through the roof because people played for the team—not just for themselves—and were intolerant of a half-hearted effort. They were self-monitoring. They dealt swiftly with members who disregarded the team's rule system, whether those rules were written down or just implicitly agreed upon by all. They gave generously to the player who had the "hot hand."

Perhaps even more important than getting the right people into key executive positions is easing executives out of those positions in a timely manner. As business demands change quickly, different talents are needed in top jobs every few years. However, once in a top position, executives are seldom eager to leave, even when business needs change. A growing issue for succession planning is finding better ways to get people out of top jobs more readily without relying on the expensive buyout approaches of the past.

CHAPTER 10

TEAM WORKS

Build the team to get the win

Manteo Mitchell was a dedicated team player in the 2012 summer Olympics, yet he competed in an individual sport. He redefined the phrase "carrying an injury" when it was revealed he ran the 4x400 meter relay race with a broken leg.

Mitchell ran the first leg and helped the United States finish as joint fastest qualifiers for the final as they and the Bahamas team were given identical times of 2:58.87. An x-ray confirmed he had broken his left fibula bone during his run. Manteo Mitchell got the baton from US teammate Tony McQuay and was hurting badly. Mitchell said: "As soon as I took the first step past the 200m mark I felt it break. I heard it. . . It felt like somebody literally just snapped my leg in half. I knew if I finished strong, we could still get it (the baton) around. I saw Josh Mance motioning me in for me to hand it off to him, which lifted me. I didn't want to let those three guys down, or the team down, so I just ran on it." Though it hurt badly, he had to continue for his team. He was amazed that he split forty-five seconds on a broken leg.

USA Track and Field chief executive officer Max Siegel added: "Manteo has become an inspiration and a hero for his teammates. Without his courage and determination to finish, Team USA would not be at the starting line in the final. What a team player."

So, too, did teamwork blossom for U.S. Women's Gymnastics in the 2012 Summer Games. Each of the five gymnasts brought something unique and important to the team. It has been said that team captain Aly Raisman brought experience, having already competed at several international events. And though not always the highest scoring, she was skilled in all areas. By contrast, vaulter McKayla Maroney competed in just one event but was considered the best in the world.

Jordyn Wieber was highly regarded for her consistency in competition. Though she did not qualify for the all-around competition, she did recover to achieve strong performances the next day, helping to push her team to the top. The youngest of the group, Kyla Ross, lacked experience but demonstrated grace under pressure—especially on the uneven bars. Finally, there was sixteen-year-old Gabby Douglas. Her previous competitive record made some people wonder whether she could handle the pressure of the Olympics. Her performances in both the team finals and the all-around competition silenced those doubters. The individual strengths of these five athletes, when brought together, were truly golden.

First and foremost, the gymnasts had a **team-first** mind-set. Before each went up to perform, her teammates could be heard delivering encouragement and praise. After each performance, spectators saw hugs and high-fives from her teammates. Indeed, the whole was greater than the sum of its parts. Are you doing enough with your team to build a whole greater than the sum of its parts?

As another example, competitive sailing is not a spectator sport. Every person on board has a vital role to play. All share in the work and in the rewards. Sailing requires a strong, cohesive, and well-oiled team. Tactician, navigator, sail trimmer, and skipper have their respective roles and responsibilities: one concentrates on how wind shifts affect the boat; another provides information about where they are in relation to the next mark; one watches for signs of wind hundreds of yards away and tries to identify its strength and direction; and the skipper serves as the integrator, coach, champion, and motivator. A friend of mine of four decades engages in competitive sailing. His team medaled sailing from Seattle to Hawaii a few summers ago, and he regarded their teamwork and the team's work as a thing of beauty.

Throughout my career, I have been privileged to work with successful "captains" who distinguish themselves by their ability to tap, orchestrate, and utilize the talents and skills of "crew members." A common characteristic is their ability to listen to others and to consider their opinion. They made other people—sometimes many levels below them in the hierarchy—feel important. They promoted a stronger, more cohesive, and more synergistic team, marked by the shared responsibility, alignment of purpose, effective communication, and rapid response…the wellsprings of spirited performance.

Teamwork combines motivation, commitment, inspiration, and leadership to get people working together as one.

In the end, it's all about the competitive edge: the commitment, the pursuit, the achievement. It is one thing to try when there's no risk of failure, but quite another to put it all on the line and challenge the impossible. To unlock human potential, high-performing teams have created many tools, each building on past knowledge, keeping the proven, discarding the superfluous, and incorporating innovations. Theirs is a continuous search for excellence.

Set team performance objectives: clarify each team's mission, objectives, strategy, and tactics; identify each team's distinctive competencies and centers of excellence; surface the problems, issues, and barriers to completing the mission; and identify areas of overlap/white spaces and resolve or eliminate.

To achieve goals, work with team leaders to articulate a mission, identify key result areas for which they are responsible to lead/support, explain strategies needed to achieve desired outcomes, and develop tactics to support those strategies. Each team member then identifies and conveys the changes desired to enable their team to achieve its

Accept nothing less than 100 percent truth, 100 percent trust, 100 percent accountability, and 100 percent effort.

objectives—including activities to import from other teams or export to other teams. Identify productivity anchors and non-value-added activities that impede achieving critical tasks and issues that erode morale.

To build real teamwork, accept nothing less than 100 percent truth, 100 percent trust, 100 percent accountability, and 100 percent effort. The team's goal is to act in ways that help team members to: communicate and share information candidly and openly with each other; cooperate and collaborate within and across teams; value individual differences in style, perspective, and background; share successes and failures and learn from each other; take on responsibility for helping others by being dependable, reliable, and contributing fully to the team; recognize and reward individual and team accomplishments; participate in setting and communicating goals; and, last, to forge relationships with colleagues based on trust and respect, regardless of level.

Great organizations develop leaders at every level who are accountable for achieving results and exemplifying values. Leaders inspire, foster collaboration, and turn vision and strategies into action with focused, clear goals. Effective leaders coach, relay good news and bad, and give feedback that works. They show self-awareness, accept feedback, and continuously develop. Leaders speak with one voice and eliminate busy work. People are measured on the results they achieve against goals they helped to create.

Teamwork combines special forces—motivation, commitment, inspiration, and leadership—to get people working together as one. Once that force is in action, the team is virtually unbeatable. Organizations scoring high in teamwork and participation know that their mission is accomplished only through the dedication, input, and creativity of people working together to achieve clear objectives.

Successful teams are those in which: cooperation is emphasized; people are encouraged to help one another; everyone is made to feel like an important part of the team; members work together toward common objectives; the organization structure facilitates collaborative effort; people openly discuss work responsibilities; team members know how their work relates to others; and a culture is created in which others feel free to pitch in when someone is having trouble getting work out.

Early in my career, it was my privilege to work with the executive teams of some of the most powerful organizations in the world and to lead their strategic team-planning quarterly retreats. Usually lasting two to three days, these intensive executive retreats accelerated the development of a team strategy that clarified vision, leveraged strengths, and aligned the organization with its priorities.

Follow-up sessions provided participants the opportunity to learn from their experience in implementing organizational change. Through this review, deeper insight into the organization's challenges and one's own approach to problem-solving was developed. Participants identified improvement realized, uncovered blockages and impediments, and developed strategies to overcome these obstacles.

These quarterly strategy sessions were designed to accelerate the pace of change in thinking and action. By all accounts, they succeeded. When leaders train together and work together, a firm foundation for the effective management of an organization is created. People become motivated. Confident. They learn mutual respect. And they certainly become more able communicators because they understand people better. That ability is taken back to the job—where, daily, participants enjoy increased personal productivity and help others do a better job. Teams work! This was the case thirty-three years ago. It is still the case. In **Point of View 2015**, Chief Executive Officer Kevin Connelly of elite search firm Spencer Stuart notes, "*In simpler times, the success of a business could be closely linked to the intelligence, management skills and charisma of its top leader. Today, however, amid much more dynamic, faster-moving marketplaces, disruptive technologies and changing customer preferences, organizations require more than a great leader and a sound strategy. They require high-performing leadership teams able to collectively solve complex business challenges and a culture that supports the business strategy and ignites the potential of individuals throughout the organization.*"

CHAPTER 11

FOCUS ON ESSENTIALS

Growth is the way to success

In a world where diets and diet metaphors abound, companies have been obsessed in recent years with trimming away the fat, getting lean, and shedding weight. However, many companies and industries are evidencing an overreaction that diminishes the very competitiveness they seek to preserve. In their obsession to cut costs (and people), some companies cut too close to the bone, leaving themselves with insufficient human resources to serve customers or to generate new customers and revenue. They suffer corporate anorexia.

Yes, some companies need to reduce staff, cut costs, and rationalize activities. You may need to restructure and reengineer, de-layer the organization, make it flatter, reengineer processes, and improve response time. The results of such efforts can be seen on the bottom line, with vastly improved financial performance.

That said, future success can't depend on restructuring or reengineering alone. If you have cut much fat in recent years, further cost cuts and process improvements are unlikely to have much impact on profit margins. Your financial success will depend more on restoring growth: to innovate, seek the right markets, to be highly competitive, adapt quickly to change, and to generate growth.

A generation of managers has devoted their attention to continuous improvement, quality control, and making companies smaller and more efficient. But they may focus their efforts so much on gaining efficiencies that they obscure their vision of new possibilities for future growth.

A lean staff is not always more entrepreneurial; cutting workers does not always reduce bureaucracy or open up lines of communication. Often the opposite occurs.

Downsizing often creates more barriers than it eliminates, and companies cut the very initiatives in R&D, brand management, and human capital needed for growth. With heads down and people focused more on *keeping* their jobs than *doing* their jobs, suffering resentment if let go but guilt and exhaustion if kept on, there is little innovative thinking.

Expansion/contraction cycles happen. Every bull market has been followed by a bear market, and every bear market has been followed by a bull market.

Seemingly never-ending downsizing and a focus on cost reduction rather than growth spreads disillusionment. People grow weary of agreeing to goal packages predicated upon adequate resources, only to have the resources pulled away while they are still held accountable for accomplishing the same objectives. Staff members become expert at restructuring, and as a result, a certain bunker mentality dominates their thinking. This mentality enables needed changes in the function's cost structure, but it also creates a climate where new initiatives and opportunities are not pursued. The old axiom is still true: "You can't save your way out of a recession—you can only invest your way out." Smart bets, new focus, lean structures and systems, and flawless execution are the answer—not just cost reduction and a bunker mentality.

We will likely experience continued turbulence, new regulatory challenges, and lingering economic uncertainty. Thus, success will depend on speed and competitiveness to capitalize on fast-moving changes in markets, technologies, and the business landscape. Winning companies will anticipate, drive, and capitalize on change in the quest for ever-higher performance. They will be ruthless at pruning underperforming people, customers, processes, and product lines, but they will always leverage their strengths. Competitive advantage will go to the company that builds on its strengths—championing change, generating innovative solutions, reinventing the business model, and competing successfully. It will not go to the company that hides, reacts, bounces from crisis to crisis, or does not hold to its vision. High-performing companies invest in critical areas in bad times as well as good—and they will shoot to the head of the pack when the recovery comes.

Instead of mandating across-the-board cuts, focus on work that really matters. Rather than reduce R&D, cut marketing, shrink human capital initiatives, try working aggressively to overthrow systems and structures that don't support the vision. Reduce excessive paperwork, redundant or inhibiting support functions, excessive reports, presentations, and meetings. With overlap and duplication minimized and non-value-added work reduced, you can increase your investment in R&D, brand-building, marketing, and human capital—the sources of sustainable competitive advantage. Trimming fat accomplishes more when you are simultaneously building muscle.

Every downturn can also be an opportunity to improve strategy, management, and execution. Winning companies out-hustle and out-maneuver the competition. They create and hold to a clear vision for the future direction of the business and ensure that activities and efforts are focused, consistent and driven by the vision. So, when you are tempted to react to a downturn with across-the-board cuts, or cuts into the lifeblood of growth, rather than mortgage the future to pay for the present, raise your voice in opposition.

ANTICIPATING CHANGE

The essence of competitive advantage

Anticipating and preparing for change is the essence of competitive advantage. While every leader plans and communicates their strategy before the competition begins, once in the race, it's often necessary to make split-second decisions to redirect efforts.

If you don't notice the shifts in the wind and adjust quickly, you may lose your strategic options. Since opportunities come and go rapidly, you can quickly become a victim of changing circumstances. You couldn't watch the 2012 Summer Olympics without being inspired by each athlete and their story.

Michael Phelps' comeback in the 2012 Olympics was nothing short of astounding. The two individual medley races between Phelps and Ryan Lochte were heavily anticipated. For Phelps, however, the first stage of the competition was very disappointing.

For only the second time in his entire Olympic career, Michael failed to earn a medal. He finished fourth, well over 4 seconds behind Lochte, who lived up to the buzz accorded him right away and earned a Gold medal. People questioned whether Phelps was still one of the world's best swimmers. Perhaps the sun had begun to set on his career.

Phelps, like virtually all Olympians, had a plan to keep on track. He kept his cool and did not veer off course. Leveraging the sleekness of his long and powerful upper body, he stretched out, extending his arms, legs, and torso, and made up for lost ground in spectacular fashion.

Like Olympic athletes, most business professionals have to think not only in the present, but the future as well. Michael Phelps admitted, "I can't remember the last day I didn't train." It is incumbent on each of us to constantly stretch, push ourselves, learn new concepts, and rethink old assumptions.

When Phelps prepares for a race, he has a laser-like focus. At this level, all the athletes must be 100 percent focused or there will be no run for a medal. Olympic athletes stay focused on results and set clear objectives for every workout.

And past Olympic performances are no guarantee. Just ask Phelps. He knew coming in to this Olympics that the pressure was enormous. I enjoyed his quote: "I know it won't be eight medals again. If you want to compare me to that, that's your decision, not mine. I'm going out there to try to accomplish the things that I have in my mind…and in my heart."

Olympic athletes may train all their lives, but their window for competing is quite short. There is always someone trying to beat them with a new technique, strategy, or style. They are the best at what they do because of their discipline, focus and hard work, and ability to adapt to changing conditions. This is true for all of us.

Phelps swam with Lochte in earning a Silver medal on the 4x100 meter freestyle competition and a Gold medal in the 4x200 meter freestyle. After breaking the medals record, he set his sights on redemption in the 200-meter individual medley, where he had another chance to beat Lochte. This time, Michael Phelps was ready. He was at his best, and he evened the score with Lochte with a Gold-medal victory. Phelps was in the lead for the entirety of the race and proved he could still be the world's best individual-medley swimmer.

With this win, Phelps not only took a Gold medal back from Lochte, but became the first male swimmer in Olympic history to win the same swimming event in three consecutive Games. For the second straight race, Phelps had done something no one had ever done before, while also winning his sixteenth Gold and twentieth medal in what was quite possibly his biggest win of the Games. He won over his biggest competitive rival, Ryan Lochte. Ah, redemption is sweet!

Thriving on challenge…anticipating and mastering change. The four Golds and two Silver medals he won in the 2012 Games upped his lifetime Olympic medal total to twenty-two medals. He is the most decorated Olympian in history.

EMBRACING CHANGE

Every business faces a future in which the only certainty is change: the rush of new technologies, increasingly demanding customers, changing values and skills of the workforce, and increasing complexity in the global marketplace.

Anticipating and preparing for change is the essence of competitive advantage. Developing the mind-set and ability to do this is a formidable challenge. Organizations have established ways of doing things.

Business flows in cycles: bulls follow bears; bears chase bulls. There is opportunity to enhance one's competitive position in every phase of those cycles. Successful companies and leaders constantly search for market opportunities/threats and take quick, creative action. You can feel the organizational pulse rate by the speed with which they commit to action, allocating and reallocating resources (time, talent, and capital) to pursue opportunities. Decisions are made quickly, and vision is translated into action. People are recognized and rewarded for these practices. However, as noted in significant research, many companies cannot *seize* opportunities prompted by change because they cannot see opportunities that derive from that change. They are so busy making the most of yesterday's opportunities, they cannot see today's or create tomorrow's.

Leaders and organizations often understand intellectually that they must let go of practices that no longer work. But they are in cognitive prisons, built on faulty logic, thinking, "If it worked before, it should still work now. Shouldn't it?" Business conditions change dramatically and they do not react! Rather than recognize and adapt to new conditions, they may actually try harder than ever with the *old* playbook, despite the reality that the game has changed.

Developing the mindset and ability to embrace change is a considerable challenge. World-class competitors can do it. They know that change is accelerating and that in a time of constant change, the ability to learn and change faster than their competitors is a competitive advantage. The structure, communications, processes, and rewards are riveted to support the new direction.

Many excellent companies have fallen from grace, not because they ignored their customers or lacked superb management skills, but because business conditions shifted and they failed to adapt. With fluctuating markets, proliferating technologies, and changing political frontiers, the challenge is no longer to manage growth. Now managers must cope with sudden shifts in the rules of the game. Are you prepared? How will you handle sudden and radical changes in business conditions that create business discontinuities or break points?

The pace and complexity of change will only increase. Time has compressed, and windows of opportunity have narrowed. Continuing change and dynamic pressures appear to be the only certainties for the future.

Changes can come from out of the blue. Traditional competencies or market niches can be challenged by new technologies, generating new skills and new products. We see:

- Faster research and development in technology, speeding up product obsolescence.
- Faster competition, because a pioneer's time advantage is shrinking, and fast-followers do not incur the high research and development costs that the innovator must amortize.
- Faster market segmentation, because rather than the mass market of the past, we now have a rapidly changing society of many different groups.
- Faster market saturation, because the internet, mass distribution and communication speed up the creation and availability of new products and services.

How well organizations adapt to new conditions will determine who will survive and who will thrive. Those that succeed will meet the challenge, respond quickly and surely to new opportunities, and remain competitive in an era of accelerated change.

CAPITALIZING ON CHANGE

The 1990s were good to business—the wind was at the back of many who took full advantage of boom times. Then the good times stopped in the 2000s. Tailwinds turned to headwinds as the past years saw an unprecedented global financial meltdown. Businesses of all kinds were adversely affected by slowing sales, falling volumes, and increasing pressures on the global economy. There was a continuing shake-out of firms that had expanded their operations in the boom markets. Market conditions became increasingly challenging.

Many key players folded their tents and went out of business. Others simply withdrew from the business and redeployed assets in favor of more traditional services. During challenging times, many players hunkered down and just tried to hold on.

However, the best companies and leaders use these cycles to build on to their position. Despite the headwinds, or perhaps because of them, companies like Apple, Ford, and Merck continue to position themselves for robust growth in market share and earnings.

While industry competitors were shifting into a defensive mode, trying hard not to lose, exceptional companies focused on playing offense, trying to win, even dominate.

Change in today's business landscape is constant and unpredictable—its speed is a blur. The effect can be either positive or unsettling, and it takes agile, flexible leadership to navigate these waters. The market is moving, so organizations need to move quickly. Skill-set obsolescence, turf struggles, inward focus, lack of innovation, slow decision-making… these should be avoided at all costs.

Those with the leading edge clearly had plans. Market swings and industry ups and downs would not put them on hold. It was as if those leaders felt, "Our continued success depends on our ability to face and address our challenges decisively. We have seen downturns before and each time emerged stronger and with greater market share. But success will depend upon our ability to react quickly in adjusting and adapting to changing market conditions, and to continue aggressively pursuing all opportunities to enhance and strengthen our business model."

These leaders seize the opportunities prompted by change, and rather than halt, they accelerate efforts to select, develop, motivate, and mobilize high-performing teams. A business rises and falls on the strength of its talent. Talent creates the platform for growth as the ultimate source of competitive advantage.

All change begins with a mandate for change. In business, external competitive market forces, changes in industry and product structure, a radically changed business climate, or business-specific events can all serve as trigger events for implementing change. Most successful change begins with a business-driven sense of urgency—the recognition and identification of a compelling reason and the successful mobilization of change variables.

You either shape the future, or the future shapes you! You can choose how you will face change. You can lead or be led by change. You can dodge, resist, and avoid change while trying to survive, or you can anticipate, promote, and lead change to your advantage. Your success depends upon which path you choose. Which path will you chose?

Choose to move proactively! See and seize opportunities prompted by change. Don't be so busy making the most of yesterday's opportunities that you fail to make the most of today's or create tomorrow's opportunities.

Most companies wait too long to attempt transformations, doing so only when the signs of trouble have become glaringly obvious. However, in today's business environment, that is likely too late. High performers, by contrast, change before they must, knowing the best way to change is from a position of strength.

In 2002, Fujio Cho, then President of Toyota Motors, launched a change initiative called Global Vision 2010. On one level, it was a surprising move. At the time, Toyota was not only Japan's largest automaker, it was the third

You either shape the future, or the future shapes you!

largest in the world, with the most envied balance sheet in the industry. Cho's reason for shaking things up when business was so strong? "Any company not willing to take the risk of reinventing itself is doomed," he said. "The world today is changing much too fast." In today's environment, once the signs of trouble have become evident, it is likely too late.

You have to manage differently, more creatively. Generate a continuous flow of new, practical, and usable ideas. New ideas are needed to increase efficiency in systems, policies, and procedures; to create more economical and effective ways of operating; to tackle intractably stubborn and costly problems; to develop new products, processes, and services; and to market them.

Success is the result of seeing and seizing opportunity. Change creates new and attractive opportunities. Since several players will seek to seize these new opportunities, identifying and seizing opportunities quickly is essential. Success today will not become success tomorrow without continual adaptation of strategy, style, and speed to a changing environment. So look ahead to the challenges of the future. Change cannot and will not be arrested. You must change and adapt just to stay in the game. Change can be disruptive, pervasive, and fast. Change will test your strategies, operations, and structures.

Expect resistance to change. It will happen especially:

- When the purpose of the change is not communicated clearly. Mystery and ambiguity do not add to the excitement.

Instead, they cause suspense and anxiety. Fear of change is disruptive.

- When people affected by the change are not involved in the planning of change. People often don't like changes made *to* them, but don't mind changes made *by* them. We support that which we help create. When people can voice their opinion and are heard, acceptance is more likely.
- When culture, habits, or customs are ignored, resistance will occur.
- When there is poor communication. Disseminate information broadly and deeply about the change to all constituents to dispel insecurity and promote cooperation.
- When there is fear of failure. No one wants to fail. If possible failure is perceived and the known outcome of failure is "punishment," resistance will occur. Reassurance of sufficient time, resources, and training to adjust to the change will help relieve resistance.
- When the cost is too high or the reward inadequate. If the change won't satisfy certain needs—higher status, higher pay, psychic rewards—resistance occurs. People can then quit and leave—or worse, they can quit and stay.

Failure to anticipate resistance to change can be costly. A sobering example: Due to his success at Apple and Target, retail superstar Ron Johnson was hired as CEO by J.C. Penney in November 2011. He was hired to shake up the store's stodgy image and attract new customers. After being hired, Johnson tapped another Apple Store veteran as COO.

The new leadership endeavored to update the chain with more trend-conscious merchandise and revamp its outmoded operating systems. They decided to eliminate sales events and discount coupons and engaged in other initiatives.

Many initiatives that made the Apple Store successful, such as the "full but fair price" concept, did not work at J.C. Penney and ended up alienating its aging customers, who were used to heavy discounting. Alas, this sparked a massive shopper exodus. The company went into freefall, becoming one of the most dramatic failures in retail history.

On April 8, 2013, Mr. Johnson was let go as the CEO of J.C. Penney and replaced by his predecessor. Alas, Ron Johnson was known as an exceptional executive. That said, he tried what had worked before for him. When it didn't work, he doubled down. He may have succeeded if he instituted radical changes more slowly. Perhaps time was running out. We will never know. Key lesson: be sure to pace and communicate change.

Seize opportunities prompted by change. While you can't avoid change, you can choose how you'll face it. You must understand the many changes affecting you, exploit them, and profit through the experience to produce breakthroughs in customer service, innovation, productivity, and quality.

The best leaders seem to sense which task merits the highest priority, seize the initiative, and devote enormous energy to finishing. They are dogged in their pursuit of goals, while maintaining the flexibility to change as the situation develops.

Companies with high-performance cultures judge themselves by anticipating events rather than *reacting* to them. They know that gaining and maintaining a competitive advantage is a constantly moving target. They know how to keep moving, adapt quickly to meet market changes, and always stay on the leading edge. To win, you must not only anticipate change, but shape it. World-class competition provides people and companies with opportunities to exhibit extreme physical, emotional, intellectual, and psychological courage. Competitive events reflect a basic struggle—it's survival of the fittest.

The best leaders and organizations choose to move proactively. They judge themselves and their people by the ability to gain and maintain a competitive advantage. You gain advantage by being more responsive and flexible. You compete nimbly with time, grab advantage by bringing products or services to market faster than rivals, keep moving, adapt quickly to meet market changes, and always stay on the cutting edge. Will you move proactively?

DON'T WAIT...ANTICIPATE

A decade ago, a consulting firm touted its services with the following mantra: "Some watch. Some wait. Some pounce." The titans of business, like the masters of sport, know that anticipating and preparing for change is the essence of competitive advantage. Success is the result of seizing opportunity before your competitors or adding significant value. Change creates new opportunities. Several players will seek to seize these new opportunities. Identifying and seizing opportunities quickly is essential for future growth.

The best competitors adapt quickly to meet market and technology changes and always stay on the cutting edge. Instinct and anticipation put them in the right place at the right time to make the play.

This principle of anticipation is so often overlooked or completely ignored. Many leaders know that they must let go of practices that do not work. But they are imprisoned by old habits. Successful companies and leaders know when to move on. Like the trapeze artist, they know that to get to the next bar, they must let go of the bar they are on. You cannot get to second base without first leaving first base. Of course, letting go of the status quo isn't easy. But world-class competitors get on with it. They know that the pace of change is accelerating, and their source of competitive advantage is the ability to learn faster than competitors and improve execution.

The past, it seems, is prologue. If you are not ahead of the threat, you're reacting to it. Anticipating and preparing for change is the essence of competitive advantage.

Some watch. Some wait. Some pounce…Most WAIT!

Change requires people to do new things while their experience, training, and compensation programs support the old things. An organization's investment in the status quo is always heavy. So they wait, always needing more time, data, or resources.

The source of competitive advantage is a constantly moving target. Yet people and organizations are lulled into complacency, reacting to events rather than creating their desired future. For example, people often buy burglar alarms *after* they have been burgled. The same system might have prevented the burglary in the first place. People commence diets and exercise programs *after* they are diagnosed with a serious health issue. The same discipline would have prevented the ailment in the first place. Insurance agents speak of huge increases in sales of earthquake insurance immediately *after* an earthquake.

Jural Aviv, Golda Meir's bodyguard and Israeli agent upon whom the movie *Munich* was based, also advises us to ensure our anticipation strategy factors in the changing dynamics of the threat.

Some watch. Some wait. Some pounce…Most WAIT!

For example, our airport technology and Transportation Security Administration (TSA) systems are outdated. We look for metal, yet the new explosives are made of plastic. A lunatic tried to light his shoe on fire. Because of that, now everyone has to take off their shoes. So a group tried to bring aboard liquid explosives. Now we can't bring liquids on board. Many of our strategies are reactive. We must anticipate and be proactive.

Forbes magazine states, "If you are not ahead of the threat, you're reacting to it." Examples of anticipation abound. Former ice hockey great Wayne Gretzsky was quoted as saying, "I do not go where the puck is…I go where the puck will be."

The NBA championship Chicago Bulls of the 1990s were constantly passing to each other without looking. They simply anticipated where their teammate would be.

In baseball, the fielders move at the crack of the bat. Instinct and anticipation place them in the right position to field the ball.

You either shape the future, or the future shapes you! You choose how you will face change. You can lead or be led by change. Your success depends upon which path you choose. So move proactively. How? You can:

1. Look in and learn about your practices;
2. Look out and learn about the best practices of others;

3. Look ahead and scope out opportunity; and

4. Take action by moving, executing, and always raising the bar.

You can stand still and get buried by the avalanche—or learn to ski. In other words, those who do not learn from the mistakes of the past are destined to repeat them.

So it is true in business. To win, today's executives must not only anticipate change, but shape it. The challenge is to recognize and adapt to change before a crisis. Exceptional people are able to do just that. They have a striking capacity to institutionalize change. They never stand still. Moreover, they seem to recognize that they have internal strengths that can be developed as conditions change.

When I taught in the University of California, Berkeley executive program entitled "Managing in the Global Economy," one of my executive groups was led by a prominent CEO. He stood and addressed the participants and said, "Anticipating and preparing for change is the essence of competitive advantage. No other exceeds it. No other equals it."

Wise observation.

CHAPTER 13

INNOVATING INNOVATION

Encourage innovation

In the Olympics, athletes must never simply perfect old stunts, but rather perfect new stunts, many of which have never been done before. This is especially true for gymnastics. Until recently, each gymnast competed in both compulsory and optional exercises. Compulsories made up an exact routine that had to be followed without variation. Each routine was composed of individual maneuvers called "tricks." In the optional exercises, routines must follow some guidelines, but the gymnast is free to incorporate his or her own tricks.

For this analogy, we go back to the Olympic Games in Los Angeles in 1984. As winner of two Olympic Gold medals, Peter Vidmar notes, "If a gymnast performs a perfect routine, he will score a 9.4. Then additional points can be added for risk (.2), originality (.2), and virtuosity (.2), to bring the total to 10.0. Points are deducted for slipping, hesitating, or falling. Falling, for example, usually takes at least .5 away from someone's score."

A good performance involves both power and technique. According to Vidmar, "In floor exercise, for example, you have to work on your takeoff angle, how far your body's going to be above the floor, how much power you have going into the floor, whether or not you can rebound off the floor or whether your legs absorb some of that power. Sometimes it will take months or years to figure out what you should have done."

Clearly, the sport's evolving at a very fast pace. Athletes must look at trends and try to think of things before someone else does. According to Gold medalist Peter Vidmar, "You'll go to an international competition and see the Russians do a crazy trick. So you go back to the gym and learn it in a week and think, wow, if I'd known they were going to do that I could have learned it too. The whole point is to be ahead and not play catch up. The countries that win are the countries setting the pace."

Innovation is the lifeblood of any business. Whether it is a groundbreaking invention or an incremental change in process or structure, innovation is about generating new ideas that will give the company's products and services a competitive edge. Business must constantly renew, reinvent, and reinvigorate. In today's challenging economic environment, it may be tempting to scale back, but it is actually more important than ever to innovate. Innovation lies at the heart of profitable growth.

Most successful innovations follow a basic, predictable pattern. Learn the principles behind this pattern, and unleash the power of innovation in your organization. The principles of innovation don't flow solely from today's world of Apple, Google, and Facebook. Many of the same principles were employed for decades—from the 1920s through the 1980s—by Bell Labs, one of the most innovative scientific organizations in the world. I lived a mile from its Bell Labs research and development facility in Holmdel, New Jersey, and stories of innovation emanating from Bell Labs were as legendary then as Apple's stories are now.

You tell yourself that innovation is a top priority, but between meetings, emails, and dealing with the crisis of the day, somehow you never get around to it. How do you break the cycle? How do you stop tending to the tyranny of the urgent?

First, streamline business processes—identify and eliminate productivity anchors, those bureaucratic processes that are not needed or efficient. Then reduce or get rid of non-value-added initiatives. In every organization there are legacy initiatives that no longer fit the organization's strategic direction. They are there because they were once, though no longer, important. They should be eliminated. Resolve those two issues and you'll uncover a leaner and more nimble organization that can innovate at will.

It is one thing to recognize the value of innovation but another to make it happen. Effecting change necessarily means reinventing business strategies, processes, and systems, as well as being open to pilot tests and the possibility of failure. It demands creative thinkers, fearless leaders, and a culture that embraces change combined with the capability to turn new ideas into winning products and services. No small challenge.

So how is your company doing? Is your firm leading, managing, and creating a culture for innovation, success, and business breakthroughs? To stay ahead of the curve, organizations must redefine the rules and build a culture for innovation. What is the secret that allows some companies to distinguish themselves in the way they encourage, recognize, and reward new ideas?

I cannot locate a single mold out of which innovative companies are forged. However, they tend to share some similar characteristics. In no small measure, the secret is their *willingness to fail*. Many companies tout their risk-taking predilections. However, risk, by definition, means you win some and you lose some. The real test is how the company responds to a loss or failure. Smart tries should not be punished, no matter what the outcome. There is a folkloric story that has been long illustrating this point. The story goes that Thomas Edison failed more than one thousand times when trying to create the light bulb. When asked if he felt like a failure, Edison allegedly said, "I have not failed a thousand times. I have successfully discovered a thousand ways how NOT to make a light bulb."

However corny the story, the principle is relevant and sound. The idea is that even if you try and fail, it doesn't mean you didn't learn something.

What are the new tools that enable companies to harness an explosion of new and innovative ideas in a changing world? Steps one and two are described above. Just cut through the clutter. Step three is to encourage the idea-generators. This is paramount. These are the leaders at all levels who champion change, generate innovative solutions, and thrive on innovation, encouraging risk-taking and diversity of perspectives.

Throughout your organization are idea-generators with new ideas for stimulating productivity, improving quality, reducing cost, or enhancing business practices. It might be that someone in manufacturing has a unique idea for advertising, while someone in human resources may have new approaches to customer service. Capture those ideas.

Idea-generators envision new possibilities and embed them in your organization's culture and practices. As a result, your company differentiates itself from competitors, workers are motivated to excel, retention is high, and business performance skyrockets.

CULTIVATING IDEA-GENERATORS

Here are some proven strategies for nurturing idea generators:

Recognize them. Successful companies and leaders are constantly on the lookout for opportunities. They search for market opportunities/ threats and take quick, creative action. You can feel the organizational pulse rate by the speed with which they commit to action, allocating and reallocating resources (time, talent, and capital) to pursue new opportunities. Decisions are made quickly, and vision turns into action.

Idea generators are constantly searching. They engage in constant innovation, identifying opportunities and anticipating demand. They often gather ideas from other industries. Good idea. In other words, if you want your clothing company to cultivate exemplary customer service, have tea at the Ritz-Carlton. If you want to attract top talent, benchmark practices at Apple.

When they cultivate these ideas, they define the ideas in terms of key strategies most valued by management, be they innovation, productivity, or customer focus. Then they promote the ideas throughout the organization. When the approval is given, as it often is, they implement with precision.

Create roles for them. Create strategic nurseries, or formal units dedicated to exploring new business ideas or new ventures. Then carve out roles that leverage the strengths of these idea generators. Ensure that they land in a good position after an idea has been implemented. If idea generators are not rewarded for championing ideas, others will not do so.

Empower them. Set them loose in the organization within a clear framework. The clearer the boundaries, the more comfortable they will feel taking risks within them. Many companies have the 10 percent rule, giving people 10 percent of their time to work on projects of their own choosing. 3M was a pioneer in the practice of allocating a meaningful percentage of time for people to work on pet projects that might transform the business. Recently, LinkedIn initiated a new program called LinkedIn [in]cubator. Through the program, any LinkedIn employee can pitch a project to executives. If approved, the employee and their team get up to three months to dedicate their time and energy to realizing their vision. Though not every project will get the green light, for at least some LinkedIn workers this will be the equivalent of 25 percent of their time.

Reward them. Idea generators are motivated primarily by challenge, intellectual stimulation, and seeing ideas transformed into action. Reward them by carefully considering their ideas, visibly supporting meritorious ideas, and publicly acknowledging their achievements. Motorola, for example, annually announces new recipients of its Dan Noble Fellow Award and recognizes a broader group of valued technologists by naming them to its Science Advisory Board.

Celebrate their ideas. The single greatest factor determining whether ideas take hold in a company is perceived top-management support. Demonstrate your backing for a great idea at town hall meetings or through organization-wide memos. Management team meetings should be a forum where participants discuss how they're using the idea. At Motorola during the late '80s and the entirety of the '90s, Six Sigma quality was the first agenda item for every meeting. At McDonnell Douglas in the mid to late '80s the first agenda item for each meeting was progress on the "Five Keys to Self-Renewal," which focused on productivity, management and ethics.

CAN YOU AFFORD TO INNOVATE IN A RECESSION?

Innovation is in the DNA of every great company. The innovation process is considered a sustainable competitive advantage. It permeates all aspects of the business—innovation in product and marketing, workplace practices, and corporate governance. Creating trends. Continuously improving through change.

Now, more than ever, constant and meaningful innovation is critical to success. The worldwide business environment is fiercely competitive. Global trade, instantaneous communication, and the ease of market entry are among the forces putting greater pressure on product and brand differentiation. To be successful, it is imperative that we change, competing in new and different ways that are relevant to the shifting times. We must rethink our assumptions, reinventing and using the power of ideas for continuous improvement across all dimensions of our business, from modest improvements to total transformation.

But can you afford to innovate in a recession? Actually, you cannot afford not to. Nothing delivers more value to a business than innovation. Plot the path to innovation and your whole company wins. Curtailing innovation efforts in tough times is a long-term strategic mistake. An empty innovation pipeline increases the risk of long-term competitive disadvantage. As the economic cycle inevitably shifts upward, companies that have dropped the innovation ball will find their fortunes sagging just as the economy has a resurgence.

Research and development or other innovation-related areas are natural places to look when searching for areas to cut to meet stricter budget targets. After all, these investments are unlikely to offer immediate returns, so trimming them back won't hurt the company's ability to meet top-line revenue targets.

Assiduously avoid this temptation. It might seem like your core operations have already been cut to the bone through efficiency-related efforts in the 1990s and 2000s, but many companies still have ample resources focused on efforts that are unlikely to create long-term strategic advantage. It is probably impossible to avoid a short-term crunch, so why derail your long-term competitive advantage in a misguided attempt to avoid the unavoidable?

That's not to imply you should spend innovation dollars thoughtlessly. You shouldn't. It is important to safeguard efforts with the most long-term potential, while also ruthlessly pruning efforts that aren't going to pay off.

If you want to know how to innovate in a recession, there are examples right in front of you. Success leaves clues. Watch for them. All of the obvious successes—the iPhone, iPad, Kindle, Flip, and Zipcar—have one thing in common. Their pioneers are always thinking about what's next. What's around the corner? How can we capitalize on change? Perhaps you should be thinking these things as well.

During my years at Lockheed Corporation in the early 1980s, I marveled at the model of anticipation, speed, efficiency, and innovation known as

Advanced Development Programs, or the "Skunk Works" as it was known. Abhorrent of bureaucracy and masters of anticipation, management at the Skunk Works deliberately put the Stealth fighter into production before the aircraft was perfected. They delivered several airplanes to the U.S. Air Force when still in the early phases of flight testing. As a result, the program was driven by the demands of fighter pilots rather than engineers. Further, the kind of missions flown in Iraq were already being practiced in 1982, when the first plane was delivered. This gave our servicemen a decade lead time to practice and perfect their missions before employing in the Gulf War. Sherman Mullin, who became president of the Skunk Works in 1990 upon the retirement of famed aircraft designer Ben Rich, maintains that its methods for building fabulous new flying machines have broader applications. "Even though the work we do is secret," he says, "how we do it is not secret at all."

He picked small teams of highly motivated people, gave them very tight budgets, and put them in isolation to keep senior management off their backs. "You don't let anyone in, and you give them the freedom to do their thing," he remarked. Most Skunk Works projects came in well under their budgets. Skunk Works teams prided themselves on doing projects faster and cheaper. Surprisingly, the Skunk Works technique has few emulators. Says Mullin: "Most US companies have huge amounts of unnecessary bureaucracy. The illusion is that bureaucracy brings stability and control. The fact is that it brings inertia and slowness."

An excellent prescription for success. I held a U.S. Government Top Secret Security clearance with special intelligence access while working for Lockheed. I can vouch for all of the above.

CHAPTER 14

SAY NO TO "YES MEN"

Seek out the minority opinion

U sain Bolt is the fastest man on earth, having established a number of world records. Mr. Bolt often speaks on college campuses to share his insights on motivation with a business audience and to speak about the principles for sustained success.

Bolt notes that he showed enormous early promise, but by the time he met his coach he had become an injury-prone underachiever. His coach, Glen Mills, gave him direct feedback about his strengths and weaknesses. Bolt credits much of his success to the fact that Mills was willing to take him to task when necessary. Mills told him what he **needed** to hear even if it was not what he **wanted** to hear. Mills overhauled his training program to improve Bolt's strength but also to protect a congenital spine defect that was the root cause of his recurring hamstring injuries. Further, he helped Bolt to understand that physical talent was no guarantee for success, unless accompanied by the requisite mental strength and discipline. To reach the top in any field, natural talent is a necessary, but not sufficient, condition.

It is the same for aspiring leaders who assume they will "make it" on their intellectual prowess, ambition, and talent. Finding the right coach or mentor is critical for anyone who wants to improve. So, too, is seeking, accepting, and adjusting to feedback. In a recent *Fortune* article, Google CEO Eric Schmidt stated that the recommendation to "hire a coach" was the best piece of advice he ever received—not because the coach can do it better than you, but because he or she helps you to know yourself, face your weaknesses, and decide where to allocate your efforts.

When people care passionately about doing the right thing (for customers, stakeholders, employees, and society) but disagree on how to get it done, expect to witness a creative clash of conflicting ideas as passion, energy, and emotions erupt. This is characteristic of healthy organizations. Creative synergy and spirited debate promote transformative learning, idea generation, and problem-solving.

Creative synergy and spirited debate promote transformative learning, idea generation, and problem-solving.

In unhealthy companies, such sounds are notably absent—and that's a root cause of their downfall. Indeed, silence can be deafening and deadening. Imagine a leader proposing a course of action that many direct reports feel and know to be patently wrong—yet they are silent. Their minds are racing: "Who am I to challenge the CEO? After all, he's been right many times before. His rags-to-riches story is the realization of the American dream." After much deliberation and angst, the would-be challenger keeps his thoughts to himself.

Many of these unhealthy companies were once dominant. They seemed unstoppable. Their stock prices soared, and Wall Street cheered as they delivered unprecedented returns. But lack of dissent, quiet acquiescence, and groupthink often prompted a free-fall from grace. Leadership practices were driven more by arrogance, ignorance, and greed than by a clear, noble, and compelling vision. When the dust settled, the global economy was in shambles. Little was left but broken trust and shattered lives.

In trying to conceal the impending demise, some leaders lost their way and led others astray. They began to rationalize, deceive constituents, create smokescreens, market a pipedream, and make bad business decisions. They rallied excitement, groupthink, and momentum to squelch fear and resistance. They made up their own definitions of what constituted moral, ethical, and legal behavior.

Alas, this is an oft-told tale; the confluence of arrogance, ignorance, and hubris results in a mindset of invincibility. The feeling, even certainty, that market forces would not hurt them—that they alone would endure, even dominate—permeates the culture, despite markets panicking, shares plummeting, and confidence cracking.

In times of great turbulence, people often huddle together, seeking leadership and conformity. A person voicing a dissenting opinion, negative comment, or cautious appraisal is often ostracized from the group. Non-conformity carries great risk. In stressful times, leaders rarely get objective feedback because the messenger who delivers the unvarnished truth can get killed. Thus, groupthink may permeate the organization.

This dilemma worsens due to the inherent conflict of interest when chairmen are also CEOs. The chairman is responsible for leading an independent board. The board's responsibility is to shareholders (owners). The board is entrusted with hiring, overseeing, compensating, and if necessary, firing the CEO. However, if the CEO is also the chairman, than he/she leads a board responsible for hiring, compensating, and possibly firing himself/herself. This won't happen easily, even if it's deserved. The result is often excessive compensation, job security, and limitless power. Who would dare challenge such a person?

When the need for leadership, analysis, transparency, and macro-management is greatest, we often find instead adherence to flawed strategies, a lack of healthy debate, and destruction of shareholder value. As employees tend to model the behavior at the top, these destructive practices cascade throughout the enterprise. There is often a sense of tyrannical suppression of criticism.

A healthy culture encourages dissenting viewpoints and differing perspectives. Ideas are evaluated based on the quality of the idea, not the level of the idea-generator. Such a culture might prevent the dangerous and embarrassing actions of Toyota, Countrywide, and BP. Consider this:

- In March 2014, Toyota agreed to pay a fine of $1.2 billion for concealing information and misleading the public about the safety issues behind the recalls on Toyota and Lexus vehicles affected by unintended acceleration. At least fifty-two people died in accidents from unintended acceleration caused by sticking pedals or incompatible floor mats.
- Since acquiring Countrywide, the media reports that Bank of America has paid over $100 billion to settle charges of fraud and corruption in mortgages. There is more to come. In August 2014, the Bank settled with the Justice Department for nearly $17 billion.
- BP will be forever known for the oil spill in Gulf of Mexico.

Power and money change people; they tend to rationalize, yield to fear, and cave under pressure and intimidation from superiors. But without a minority opinion, who can save the company? The ability (or lack thereof) to accept or deliver the truth is about character, choices, and courage.

Here are seven suggestions to foster creative conflict and better decisions:

1. *Create and adhere to a clear, compelling vision, set of values, and culture.* A well-developed code of values and principles provides clear standards for conduct. It presents an ethical and behavioral framework to guide responses to challenging choices. Each person is responsible to respond to situations in a manner that reflects values in action.

2. *Encourage the minority opinion.* This nourishes healthy debate and differences of opinion. In meetings, ask your staff to express their opinions before you share yours, to feel free to disagree or surface an idea that is different the others.

3. *Encourage and reward true diversity.* Diversity in every sense should be encouraged and rewarded. Embrace the diversity that can provide a different perspective, think in different ways, and contribute distinctive backgrounds to achieve goals. Select team members based on diverse styles, strengths, skills, and backgrounds.

4. *Appoint a devil's advocate when discussing agenda items.* Rotate this role to each team member. Encourage healthy debate about ideas and alternatives, but squelch personal attacks.

5. *Hold a "second chance" meeting.* Groups often rush for closure. After working an issue long and hard, they want resolution. If the team feels too good about feeling good, revisit the issue again in a week or two. This second look will enhance the quality of decisions.

6. *Create multiple anonymous feedback channels.* Enable people to state their views freely, without fear of reprisal. You might have the 2015 version of the suggestion box and bring up items from the "box" at weekly meetings (or in tweets, Instagrams, texts, email dialogues, surveys, and focus groups) and use them to stimulate discussion.

7. *Lead by example.* Walk your talk. Model candor, openness, transparency, and authenticity. In high-performing, healthy companies, you are expected to challenge the status quo; and doing so is viewed as an act of extreme loyalty. Avoid groupthink to tap individual and collective creativity and ingenuity.

Surround yourself with people who tell you what you *need* to hear, even if it is not what you *want* to hear. By doing so, you provide an example of excellence in action.

When spirited debate is required, the sound of silence can erode your effectiveness and degrade your business into oblivion. You must assiduously avoid this. Get a coach. Get someone who will tell you the truth, and tell it to you quickly.

CHAPTER 15

CULTURE COUNTS

Unite against tough competition

As a leader, you have a significant role in creating a culture that consistently elicits high performance from individuals, teams, and organizations. Ultimately, this is how you will be measured. Assess how your structure and culture impact productivity, performance, and engagement. Develop positive, constructive strategies to narrow the gap between the present culture and the ideal culture.

Toward the end of his groundbreaking career, Peter Drucker, known as the "father of management," often said, "The leader of the past knew how to *tell*, the leader of the future will know how to ask." He was advising leaders to *ask* more, tell less. Leaders should pave the way, not block the way. They should expand choices, not reduce them. Light the way for your people. Here is a punch list of actions and strategies to consider…

A high-performance culture (HPC) is a differentiator. Anticipating and preparing for change is the essence of competitive advantage. Companies with HPCs judge themselves by anticipation rather than reaction time. Gaining and maintaining a competitive advantage is a constantly moving target. Don't get stuck with a single simple notion of your source of advantage. Keep moving, adapt quickly to meet market changes, and stay on the cutting edge. To win, you must not only anticipate change, but shape it. Amazon.com founder and Chairman Jeff Bezos' recent decision to buy the *Washington Post* exemplifies this principle. In one bold stroke, he catapulted the company to a new frontier and reminded the world of his bold vision.

To create a high performance company, you must create an energizing vision and sound strategy that empowers structure and a talented leadership team. Design a total system of improvement to align these key elements. Create a leadership program that focuses on creating a world-class institution.

Learn new strategies for promoting a culture that supports the quest for excellence in anticipating and exceeding customer needs, reducing cycle time, creating flawless product and service integrity and reliability, creating cost-competitive advantage, and developing best-in-class partnerships with employees, suppliers, and customers.

For thirty years, my teams have seen a clear correlation between the "Best Places to Work" and HPCs. Harness and focus the talent, energy, intellect, and innovation of people on the common goal of winning. Give them the tools to succeed and they will stay if recognized.

Context. A strong strategic vision gives you the will to achieve your strategy, but culture provides the way. Your culture should be conducive to achieving your strategy. The context—people, systems, structures, and culture—determines which strategies are likely to work. The context also influences the strategic choices made by leaders.

Your strategy must be consistent with the context and culture. Systematic and carefully selected changes in context can be a catalyst for shifts in strategic direction.

HPCs balance strategic and operational responsibilities; reduce overlap, duplication, and confusion regarding responsibilities; and better define who plays the partner, advocate, and strategic and operational roles for specific customers. HPCs leverage distinct core competencies, reflect priorities, foster a clear charter and accountability, align key strategic resources toward the highest payoff areas, and maintain a balance between strategic versus operational focus.

Leverage distinct core competencies. Competencies are the source of competitive advantage. Competencies are the combination of skills, know-how, and resources used to compete effectively. Organizations vary dramatically in their capabilities, and in how they leverage those capabilities to achieve sustainable competitive advantage.

Capabilities should be unique, hard to replicate, and widely applicable. Unique and valuable capabilities are not easy to develop, but form the basis of competitive advantage. Identify, develop, and leverage capabilities that are specific to your organization and difficult for competitors (external/internal) to replicate. These capabilities set you apart and give you an advantage.

Align key strategic resources with your highest payoff areas. Funding of certain functions often appears to be in striking conflict with stated objectives.

Realign the structure to better support the vision. You can organize functions by business, geography, process, product, customer set, or function. Several centralized functions—executive compensation, risk, staffing, workforce diversity—are repositioned or decentralized; various top management arrangements, including "office of" options, are proposed; and roles and responsibilities are more clearly delineated. These alternatives address the issues of overlap, white space, and imbalance in provocative ways. You may wish to pursue other options. I encourage you to revisit this issue and determine the appropriateness of the current structure in satisfying your stated objectives.

A return on investment (ROI) model should govern resource allocation decisions. Uneven resource allocation often exists: mature tactical functions are funded adequately, while emerging or strategic functions typically compete for scarce dollars. Some strategic functions may be underfunded, while others are overfunded. Incremental funding requests from all sources should demonstrate their prospective impact on the business using standard measures. Only those requests with the highest impact, demonstrated in quantitative fashion, should be funded. New initiatives must also contain implementation strategies and maintenance plans for funding consideration.

Simplify systems, reduce roadblocks, and slash productivity inhibitors. Burdensome systems that inhibit productivity are contrary to the spirit and intent of transformation. Improve any budgeting process or system that is cumbersome, lacks credibility, and does not reflect major goals and initiatives. Consider the frequency, quality, and coordination of business messages.

To create a new team spirit, systems must be designed to support it. Far too often, systems and structures counter that spirit: information systems that inhibit the manager or associate from knowing the score; compensation systems that fail to differentiate between high and low performers; and structure that makes it impossible for the individual to identify with and feel part of the team or fulfill his or her charter.

Reengineer core processes. Examine the work being done and iden-tify the associated drivers; determine which activities are essential and where and how these activities should be done; recommend optimal arrangements and staffing level, mix, and deployment; modify management processes to match requirements; and develop an agenda and program for culture change (if required).

Eliminate redundant and non-value-added activities. Consolidate dispersed communication activities for synergy, better resource management, and a consistent message to employees and customers. Clearly differentiate roles and responsibilities. Eliminate some processes and activities to free up resources to reallocate to value-added endeavors.

Think of yourself as the chief transformation officer, or CTO, and articulate and champion a powerful, inspiring vision. Then, consistent with that vision, implement strategy, operational improvements, and reduce costs. Have a potent strategy for change—something unique and powerful enough to create a High Performance Organization.

Over the years, my teams and I realized that the 360° feedback clients (we had over 50,000 of them) with the highest scores in "leading change" tended to have the highest-performance work units in virtually all performance dimensions (productivity, cost, quality, AND customer satisfaction). A further truism from longitudinal research is that the leaders who treat their people best tend to have the highest customer satisfaction. Perhaps you should think more and do more about these keys to business success.

A stellar example of applying the above lessons comes from the pages of the Annual Report of Rackspace, headquartered in San Antonio, Texas. Their Annual Report of a few years ago states:

At Rackspace, we're focused on building the service leader in cloud computing. That leadership is created not by trapping customers, but by serving them so well that we generate a loyalty advantage in the marketplace. Our business economics are based on customer loyalty, and to boost that loyalty, we are constantly investing in our employees, known as "Rackers," and in our technology.

Thus, Rackspace focuses on winning this loyalty through a simple, but powerful strategy. They believe that if they take great care of their associates, known as "Rackers," their associates will in turn take great care of their customers. Satisfied customers lead to greater market share and resultant economies of scale, yielding greater profits and more satisfied shareholders.

To build a **big** company, they believe they must start by building a **great** one. So, Rackspace invests in building a great workplace, hiring great talent, and providing Rackers and customers with great technology.

The Annual Report continues,

It starts with our culture and the talented Rackers who drive our company. We're proud of being included in some of the most prestigious lists of best companies to work for in the US and the UK, because a supportive culture enables Rackers to do great work. Culture eats strategy for lunch—and culture is impossible to copy. Our culture is a competitive advantage for us. It makes it easier for us to recruit

amid today's fierce competition for technology talent, and keeps
engagement and retention levels high among our Rackers.

Many companies have verbiage like this in their documents. However, the reality often falls short of the rhetoric. That said, Rackspace is "walking the talk." Few can match Rackspace in the winning combination of business results, culture and climate surveys, retention and engagement rates, and the status often conferred upon them as one of the "Best Places to Work."

CHAPTER 16

ROLE MODEL LEADERSHIP

Trust, transparency, and credibility sustain leadership

Credibility is essential. Credibility is gained when the leader does what he says he will do. The leader must keep his promises in good times and bad. Credibility determines the actual ability to lead, the perceived ability to lead, and the integrity that causes others to place their trust in the leader. Integrity involves reliability that allows followers to know that the leader will be generally predictable. A leader who is frequently unpredictable will soon lose followers.

Many people fail in their leadership responsibilities because they have, in either a dramatic event or a series of damaging actions, lost credibility.

The leader must keep his promises in good times and bad.

Credibility is lost when executives put their own interests above the interests of their constituents: shareholders, employees, and communities. People don't give you their trust—they only *lend* it to you.

The media has widely covered leaders and institutions engaged in practices that were neither sustainable nor responsible. Former Medtronic CEO and current Harvard Professor Bill George states, "The highly visible corporate leadership failures of recent years have deeply shaken public confidence in business leaders. All too often these leaders have placed self-interest ahead of the well-being of their organizations. After the companies got in trouble, their leaders then refused to take responsibility for the harm caused to the people they served. The problems at British Petroleum, Hewlett-Packard, and failed Wall Street firms, along with the actions of dozens of leaders who failed in the post-Enron era, are glaring examples of these lapses of leadership."

I saw this up close. It was late summer 2007. Countrywide Financial Corporation was teetering and headed toward insolvency. Countrywide had emptied out ALL of its lines of credit. The company would be insolvent in days, hours, or as some said, minutes. The media reported that Founder, Chairman, and CEO Angelo Mozilo was in the process of extracting the last of hundreds of millions of his own net worth out of the company. This was done in plain sight. In fact, Countrywide's top few executives are said to have exercised nearly a billion dollars' worth of stock options while they were still hyping the company. "Pump and dump" is what the media called it. The Countrywide board approved a stock repurchase just long enough to buy back their stock at inflated prices.

It was said in the media that there was a time when people would have walked through the gates of hell for Mr. Mozilo. He was revered, held in awe. He had convinced us that we were pursuing a noble goal: housing America. But the veil of this wizard had been torn aside.

Walk behind the curtain. There wasn't much there at all: smoke, mirrors, and a litany of "trust me" and "it will be fine" assurances.

In a fit of desperation, we were told to stick with him. We were told that those who have done so before are very wealthy now. It is sad that some, though fewer and fewer, still believed him. Over time, all realized the truth. It was over. It was done.

The essence of a leader is often revealed in a matter of seconds. Often, this is during times of stress, when key decisions must be made and character is often the arbiter. This is when the character and credibility of the leader are tested. Mr. Mozilo did not pass these tests.

I wish this tale was confined to one lone institution. Alas, it is a tale about many. Earlier in my career, I had been uplifted by CEOs and other senior executives who did the right thing, the noble thing, that which took courage and commitment. However, in this instance, and for years after, I had a lens into a once-revered and now-fallen titan of commerce.

Credibility is the soul of leadership. James Kouzes and Barry Posner stated years ago that the most essential element for successful leadership is honesty, being "straightforward and fair-minded." It is no less true today.

What can we do to repair the visibly eroding standards of leadership? We must turn up the heat on our leaders. Also, we need to hold ourselves to the highest standards—because we value integrity, not because we fear legal consequences. Let's strive to be role models of leadership that exude the following leadership qualities:

- The vision to clearly define what we will do for those who depend upon us.
- The drive to share that vision broadly with those who have a stake in our success.
- The courage to question the status quo, stimulate change, and move forward.
- The ability to inspire people to action, individually and in teams.
- The foresight to empower people with new skills and stretch their capabilities.
- The wisdom to listen, learn, and translate that knowledge into stronger performance.

- The willingness to recognize and celebrate individual and team accomplishments.
- The integrity to serve as good examples through actions.

An essential element of leadership is trust. The best organizations and their leaders believe that words and deeds should match and have the strength to keep their promises through thick and thin. In translating their commitment to consistent, purposeful action, often under fire (downturn, budget crisis), the true test of leadership is passed or failed.

Without the requisite character and integrity, the organization is built to fail, not built to last.

The best leaders create trust by matching their words with their deeds and keeping their promises. Retaining outstanding people is a business imperative in both bullish and bearish times. To tackle the issues facing your industry, company, and customers, you need to take decisive action to ensure your organization is well-positioned for future success. Leaders must manage human capital more thoughtfully and proactively than ever before.

When you closely examine the core characteristics of what really makes for great leadership, it's not power, title, authority, or even technical competency that distinguishes truly great leaders. Rather, it's the ability to both earn and retain the loyalty and trust of those they lead. If you

Lead by example. Always remember, people will not believe the message if they do not believe the messenger. Character counts.

build up those you lead, if you make them better, if you add value to their lives, then you will have earned their trust and loyalty. This bond will span positional and philosophical gaps and survive mistakes, challenges, downturns, and other obstacles that will inevitably occur.

Lead by example. Always remember, people will not believe the message if they do not believe the messenger. Character counts. With it, all things are possible. Without it, all else is doomed.

ON COURAGE
AND COMMITMENT

Courage is required to stand up for what you believe. The ever-present War for Talent will be won by firms with a solid belief in the strength, capacity, and potential for growth and contribution from their people, as well as the guts and intestinal fortitude to keep their promises of development and integrity through thick and thin. This belief system includes a willingness to do the right thing for their employees, brands, the company, and society as a whole, even when personal, professional, and social risks or economic pressures confront them. This principle anchors their beliefs and behaviors today and every day. It is the navigational North Star for which I strive daily.

Such leadership in tough times takes courage and commitment! Courage is the willingness to challenge hierarchy, accepted practices, and conventional wisdom. Courage includes truth-telling and acting resolutely on your beliefs. It means standing by your convictions.

Commitment transforms a promise into a reality. Commitment is making the time when there is none, coming through time after time, year after year. It is the daily triumph of integrity over skepticism, results over activities and busy work, innovation over imitation, teambuilding over individual grandstanding, and risk-taking over mindless conformity.

Champions of new initiatives must cling tenaciously to their ideas and persist in promoting them despite frequent obstacles and imminent failures. By actively promoting the ideas—often by repeating the same arguments over and over—champions overcome (or wear down) the opposition. Inexhaustible energy is also a salient characteristic of champions. To ensure these initiatives are implemented, these leaders put themselves on the line, enthusiastically promoting change, building support, overcoming resistance, and ensuring that the change is implemented. They are motivated by a passionate belief in, and enthusiasm about, the nature of the change and what it can do.

Lead the change process, convince the skeptics, coax the uncertain, and stick with the process. Put yourself on the line, actively and enthusiastically promote change, build support, overcome resistance, and ensure that the change is implemented. Show confidence in your personal vision. Be motivated by a passionate belief in, and enthusiasm about, the change and what it can achieve.

Be a change agent who is personally dissatisfied with the status quo, create a vision of excellence, and align commitment and support to achieve

Your legacy depends upon your leadership.

that vision. Change and progress occur as a response to dissatisfaction. If you are satisfied, you have no reason to change, and you stand still. Out of dissatisfaction comes searching, change, and growth.

In managing your business and your career, balance competitive benchmarking with simply striving for your own personal best performance. Excessive involvement with competitive strategy can be distracting. The marketplace is the track, revenue is the clock, the bottom line is your record time, and the only valid role those running with you have is to spur you on to greater levels of achievement. Run your own race! Learn what customers are all about and do what you must to provide them with what they really need and want.

Be careful not to watch your competitors—the other runners—too closely, you're likely to lose your stride. If they are ahead of you, it's discouraging. If they are beside you, you can't watch them and see what's ahead. If they are close on your heels, you feel pressured. And if they are well behind you, you might be tempted to gloat. It is better to get in your own lane, take your best stride, and run your own race—from start to finish.

Your legacy depends upon your leadership. Congratulations to those of you who have already embraced the challenge of renewal and continuous improvement. Light the way, pave the way, provide clarity on priorities and values, and watch your people rise to your highest expectations.

ABOUT THE AUTHOR

With over thirty years of experience as a business leader, change agent, and organization strategist, Michael G. Winston has been in the "eye of the storm" of businesses going through massive transformation. He served in executive positions for five Fortune 100 companies (Lockheed, McDonnell Douglas, Motorola, Merrill Lynch and Countrywide Financial) across three industries (high technology, aerospace, and financial services), working on organizational strategy and performance, succession planning, leadership development, and leading change. Michael was hailed by *Leadership Excellence* as one of the "100 Most Influential Thinkers on Leadership in the World" for eight consecutive years. Michael's work has been recognized by his inclusion in many "Top Business Thought-Leaders" lists and over twenty "Who's Who" editions. He has won numerous corporate awards for exemplary performance.

Michael has delivered keynote presentations to over four hundred companies and associations and addressed executives at prestigious university executive programs too numerous to single out. He has shared the podium with Heads of State. He has also keynoted for Management Centre Europe (Belgium) several times and served as Distinguished Adjunct Professor for sixteen consecutive years at Stichting deBaak in Noordwijk, The Netherlands. Michael was named "Best Instructor" at the University of Illinois and served as adjunct professor in the graduate schools of business and management for the University of California, University of San Francisco, Golden Gate University, and Pepperdine University.

Michael's articles have appeared in *Business Week, Leader to Leader, Leadership Excellence, Business Forum, Huffington Post, Executive Excellence*, and other publications. His leadership development strategies have been utilized by such institutions as the University of Illinois Business School and executive programs. He speaks with authority because he speaks with experience.

Michael Winston holds a PhD from the University of Illinois, a Master's Degree from the University of Notre Dame, and is a graduate of executive programs from Stanford University and the University of Pennsylvania's Wharton School.

CPSIA information can be obtained
at www.ICGtesting.com
Printed in the USA
FSOW04n2127040915
10578FS